Quebec

WORLD HERITAGE CITY

DAVID MENDEL

PHOTOGRAPHS
LUC-ANTOINE COUTURIER

A VISUAL EXPLORATION OF QUEBEC CITY

This book is the first in a series of volumes that will offer an extensive visual exploration of Quebec City and its region. The author and photographer have enjoyed many exciting moments, climbing to high vantage points - and braving the elements on freezing winter days - to create images of the city that have never been seen before. We have made an effort to open doors to special places that might not otherwise be accessible, and show you details that might otherwise go unnoticed.

History is waiting around every corner, and at each site there are many layers of meaning to discover. A brief outline of the history of each major location leads to a step-by-step exploration in which general exterior and interior views are followed by photographs of selected objects, symbols and architectural elements. Texts have been kept deliberately short in order to provide as much space as possible for historic maps, images and, especially, Luc-Antoine Couturier's remarkable photographs.

There can be no substitute for actually visiting a site, or entering an historic interior. Nevertheless, the art of photography has the capacity to help us see in ways that can complement - and even surpass - the visual experience that we have when visiting a location in person. Revealed by the clarity and focus of the camera, details can be isolated and thus seen more intensely. The author and

photographer have spent many inspiring hours together, striving to create images which make accessible the beauty and meaning of each site. Returning again and again to certain places, we discovered aspects and details that we had never noticed before. In the process of preparing this series of volumes, we have both renewed our visions of the city.

For those who have visited these special places, we hope that this book will provide a souvenir. For those who have not yet travelled to Quebec, we hope that it will serve as an invitation to come here and explore this remarkable historic environment. However, this book is not only for visitors.

Few local residents have had the opportunity to enter all the interiors that are included in this volume. While the laws concerning the historic district of Quebec will probably protect the exterior appearance of most buildings, the future of many interiors remains uncertain. It is a privilege to live in this World Heritage City, but also a responsibility. The places recorded and revealed in this book are much more likely to be preserved if they are appreciated and known by the citizens of Quebec.

QUEBEC
WORLD HERITAGE CITY

In 1985, Quebec City's historic district became the first urban ensemble in North America to be declared a World Heritage Site by UNESCO. With its dramatic cliff-top location overlooking the St. Lawrence River, its fortifications, narrow winding streets and wealth of historic buildings spanning four centuries, Quebec is unlike any other city in North America.

A STRATEGIC SITE

The view from the cliff of Quebec – *Cap-aux-Diamants* – is spectacular. In the distance, looking across the St. Lawrence River towards the northeast, is the Island of Orleans, which is 34 km in length. Just beyond the island, the river opens up to become a vast estuary, leading to the Gulf of St. Lawrence and the Atlantic Ocean. When you are coming inland, from the Atlantic, it is here that the river suddenly becomes very narrow. At the

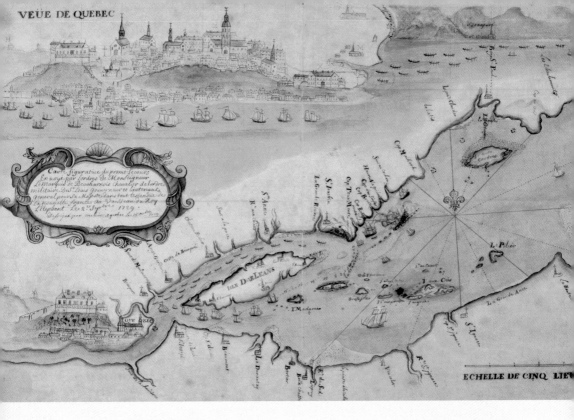

VEÜE DE QUEBEC

ECHELLE DE CINQ LIE

promontory of Quebec, the river is only about one kilometre across. This was crucial throughout much of the city's history. The name Quebec has its origin with a word in an Algonquian Indian language, meaning where the river narrows. From the cliffs of Quebec it was possible for cannons to fire across the river and, hopefully, prevent enemy ships from penetrating further west. The great cliff of Quebec, dominating the St. Lawrence from a height of more than 100 metres, makes the site a natural fortress. Located on this rocky point - jutting out into the water, somewhat like the prow of a ship - the city is surrounded by cliffs and water on all sides but one. By building a fortification wall on the western side, where there are neither cliffs nor water, it was possible to make the site almost impregnable. The walled city was besieged many times during its history, but most attacks were unsuccessful, thanks - in part - to its formidable natural defences. The French, the British and then the Americans all fought to control this very strategic location. Quebec is often referred to as the "Gibraltar of North America."

Another great advantage of this site is the depth of the river in front of Quebec. The water is deep enough that today's huge ocean liners, even those as big as the Queen Mary II, can dock right beside the lower town, even though the city is hundreds of kilometres from the Atlantic. In the past, how-

ever, it was difficult for ocean-going ships to sail beyond Quebec. The river became shallower and more difficult to navigate as you went further inland. It was only after a channel was dug in the 1840s that the larger ships could continue on towards Montreal. Until that time, they were obliged to stop and unload at Quebec, making the city a very important colonial inland port.

CAPITAL OF NEW FRANCE

Founded by French explorer Samuel de Champlain in 1608, Quebec began as a small fur-trading post, but in the 1660s, Louis XIV - the Sun King - decided to transform this little settlement into the capital of a French province in North America, *La Nouvelle France*, or New France. This French colonial empire would eventually cover much of what is now Canada and the United States, stretching as far south as the Gulf of Mexico and almost as far west as the Rocky Mountains. Quebec, the capital of the French colony, is depicted in a cartouche (right) which is included in a map of North America made in 1688 by the King's geographer in Quebec City, Jean-Baptiste Franquelin. It is a relatively accurate image of the city, although the height of the church steeples has been exaggerated, just a little bit, to impress the king.

UPPER TOWN, LOWER TOWN

Franquelin's drawing shows that the merchants' houses are located in the lower town, close to the St. Lawrence River, which along with the other waterways served as the transportation network of the time. In the upper town, protected by steep cliffs, are (from left to right) the Chateau Saint-Louis – the governor's residence, which was located close to where the Chateau Frontenac stands today – and then the religious institutions: the Ursuline Convent, founded as a school for girls in 1639; the Jesuit College, founded in 1635, one year before Harvard University; the Cathedral, Notre-Dame de Québec; and the Seminary of Quebec, founded in 1663. With the exception of the Jesuit College, which was demolished at the end of the 19th century, all of these religious institutions are still functioning in the same locations where they stood when this image was made in the 1680s. Such continuity is very rare in the North American context. Quebec is not a museum city – this is living history that has flourished over all these generations.

A VAST BUT FRAGILE EMPIRE

By the end of the 17th century the French would claim most of the continent. Quebec City was the capital of a vast, but fragile, empire with a small population to defend it, dependent on a series of forts and trading posts along the waterways and on alliances with Amerindian tribes. The English colonies were hemmed in between the Atlantic Ocean and the Appalachian Mountains. With a much larger population than that of the French, the English wanted to expand into the west – but couldn't, because they were blocked by New France. It was thus inevitable that these rival powers would come into conflict with one another in a struggle to control the continent. Despite their small numbers in North America, the French were often victorious against the English. Nevertheless, after major defeats in Europe, France signed the Treaty of Utrecht in 1713, ceding important coastal areas of North America to Britain – including Hudson Bay, with its drainage basin, Newfoundland and much of the area now occupied by Canada's maritime provinces. Nevertheless, France retained control of the St. Lawrence and the Mississippi, the two great river systems that allowed French dominance of the central part of North America.

(preceding page) Where the river narrows; map showing Quebec City and the St. Lawrence in 1724.
(below) Detail of a magnificent map that was presented to the French Court in 1688 by the King's Geographer, Jean-Baptiste Franquelin, who had travelled across the Atlantic to show his most recent maps of North America.

A WORLD AT WAR

But the Treaty of Utrecht also declared that the Iroquois Amerindians were now to be British subjects. The Iroquois territories provided access to the Great Lakes. Rivalry for the lands west of the Appalachians led to confrontation and what Winston Churchill would later refer to as the first true World War. The fighting began in 1754, with a skirmish in the Ohio country. By 1756, the "French and Indian War" in North America had evolved into the Seven Years War, spreading to Europe, India and Africa. Quebec City, the capital of New France, finally fell to the British in 1759. With the Treaty of Paris in 1763, the French relinquished control of mainland North America, keeping only the fishing islands of Saint-Pierre and Miquelon off the coast of Newfoundland, as well as their rich sugar islands in the Caribbean.

ONE OF THE GREATEST PORTS IN NORTH AMERICA

During the French regime, the port of Quebec had grown relatively slowly. The limited area available for construction in the lower town had been generally adequate for the export of furs and importation of supplies and manufactured goods for the colony. Plans were made to enlarge the port area and some landfill operations were undertaken during the 1700s, but it was not until the following century that the lower town would begin to grow rapidly.

Quebec City entered a period of rapid economic expansion during the Napoleonic Wars. When France cut Great Britain off from its supply sources for wood in the Baltic region in 1806, the British turned to their colonies and Quebec became one of the most important centres for the export of timber in the British Empire.

Fortunes were made in Quebec City as Britain's need for wood and wooden ships transformed this little colonial city into one of the greatest ports in North America during the first decades of the 19th century. The shoreline was transformed on both sides of the St. Lawrence and along the St. Charles River, as every cove was filled with wood and shipbuilders launched over 1600 square-rigged sailing vessels.

ECONOMIC DECLINE AND HARD TIMES

Quebec's expansion, however, was to slow down considerably in the second half of the 19th century. Once more, these changes had their origin with events that took place far from Quebec City. Great Britain decided to adopt a policy of free trade and removed protective tariffs that had stimulated the timber trade in Canada. To make matters

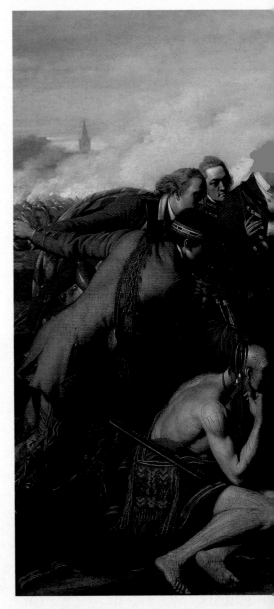

The British defeated the French at Quebec in the famous Battle of the Plains of Abraham on September 13, 1759. *The Death of General Wolfe*, by Benjamin West.

worse, the British were now making metal ships at home and no longer needed the wooden ships of Quebec. Business leaders in Canada now turned towards developing the west and building stronger links with the United States. Montreal, more centrally located, and surrounded by rich agricultural land to help with its expansion, began to take Quebec's place as the country's most important city. With the construction of canals and railways,

Montreal became the transportation and financial hub of Canada. To improve their situation further, Montreal business interests had a channel dug in the St. Lawrence so that it became possible for ocean-going ships to bypass Quebec altogether. The city of Quebec went into a period of serious economic decline.

The timber trade was big business in 19th century Quebec

A CITY PRESERVED: TRADITION AND MODERNITY

The latter part of the 19th century was a crucial time in the history of Quebec City. With hindsight, we can say that the difficult economic period that the town went through probably helped to preserve Quebec's Old City. There wasn't as much pressure to demolish and build as there was in other, more successful North American cities. Equally, if not more important, was the vision of certain key individuals who saw the benefits of preserving Quebec's rich architectural heritage.

The decline of the city did, however, lead to calls for modernization. No longer in danger of military attack, the City of Quebec requested permission from the federal government to demolish the fortifications. Demolition of the outer works, and the city gates, began in the early 1870s, and, had it not been for the intervention of the Governor General of Canada, Lord Dufferin, Quebec's fortification walls might have been lost forever.

THE FORTIFICATIONS ARE SAVED FROM DESTRUCTION

Lord Dufferin fell in love with the romantic beauty of Quebec and led a campaign to save the walls of the city. His project called for the construction of new gates, wide enough for traffic to flow through more easily. This compromise showed that it was possible to preserve important elements of the city's heritage while adapting to the changing transportation needs of a modern city.

The new gates, proposed by Irish architect William Lynn, looked nothing like the narrow military gates of Quebec's past. They were romantic structures, with towers and turrets, inspired by the defensive architecture of the Middle Ages. The evocative architecture of Lord Dufferin's project would set the tone for the construction of other picturesque, castle-like structures at the end of the 19th century, helping to redefine the city's image. Buildings such as the Military Drill Hall and, especially, the renowned Chateau Frontenac Hotel came to embody the drama and romance of Quebec's history for visitors from around the world.

The preservation of the fortifications helped to identify the area within the walls as a special place where history was considered to be important. Nevertheless, there was still no legal protection for the area. Historic buildings remained threatened and quite a few were demolished. Finally, in 1963, Quebec's Old City, including both the upper town and the lower town, was designated as a historic district. There are now laws to protect the unique character of the area and generous grants to help property owners maintain and restore their buildings.

The historic institutions of the upper town are just a few minutes' walk from one another

Lord Dufferin's project, which saved the walls of the city in the 1870s, served as an example that was to influence Quebec's evolution for generations to come. Today, as in the past, some of the most successful urban planning and architectural projects in Quebec City are based on a creative mix of tradition and modernity. There is now a general consensus that Quebec's high quality of life and economic prosperity are directly tied to the preservation of the city's human scale and historic character.

FRENCH CITY - ENGLISH CITY

Today, Quebec City is usually thought of as the birthplace of French civilization in North America, and this is certainly true, but it is often forgotten that the town was also once a bastion of the British Empire. While significant institutions, buildings and street patterns from the time of New France have survived, the vast majority of the buildings in Quebec's historic district (approximately 90%) were built after 1800, mostly in the 19th century, when British power and the example of the British way of life were in their ascendancy, not only in Quebec, but around the world.

In many ways it is the combination of British and French influences in the architecture of Quebec that makes the city unique. As we explore Quebec City and its region, we find these combined influences everywhere, from official buildings and institutions to commercial and residential architecture. For example, the typical mid-19th century house in Old Quebec is based on the tall, narrow London row house in its general dimensions and interior plan, but retains certain practical features of local French traditional architecture: steep roofs, so that the snow will slide off easily, and fire walls rising up above the roof line, to help stop the spread of flames.

This mixture of French and British influences permeates almost every aspect of our environment in Quebec City and is so familiar that it generally passes unnoticed by most of the population. Very often, however, when French-speaking Quebeckers go to Europe for the first time, they are surprised to discover that - in some ways at least - they feel more at home in London than in Paris. The language is different, but the urban environment, the houses, the institutions and the social customs are all strangely familiar. On the other hand, in Paris, the language is the same, but some aspects of the way of life feel quite foreign.

CHAMPLAIN
MONUMENT
THE FOUNDER OF QUEBEC

S amuel de Champlain, who founded a trading post at Quebec in 1608, was a man
of great determination and vision. At first he
had hoped that the St. Lawrence River might
even lead to the fabled route to the Orient. If
this had turned out to be true, the narrows in
front of Quebec might one day have served as
a lucrative control point to dominate European
trade with Asia. As he came to know North
America better, Champlain shifted his focus to
emphasize the key role that Quebec could play
as the capital of a French colony. Although
in the employ of fur-trading companies
whose first objective was to make prof-
its, Champlain saw Quebec's potential
to become the site of an important city. Working tirelessly to
explore new territories and
establish trading and military alliances with
Amerindian nations,
he used his talents
as a writer, artist
and mapmaker to
describe the north-
eastern part of this
continent.

Champlain crossed the
Atlantic more than twenty times, sparing no
effort to convince the authorities in France
to support his ambitious plans. As the King's
representative, he rose to the rank of Cardinal
Richelieu's lieutenant, with all the responsibili-
ties of a governor. Samuel de Champlain, more
than anyone else, laid the foundations for a
French colony in the New World: *La Nouvelle
France*.

This monument, which was erected in 1898 in memory of the founder of Quebec, corresponds very well with the image that we have of Samuel de Champlain as a great explorer, geographer and military leader. In fact, however, we have no idea what he actually looked like.

Champlain's statue is typical of the monuments erected in Paris at the end of the 19th century. One could even say that this it is a very Parisian monument. Paul Chevré, the sculptor, and Paul le Cardonnel, the architect who designed the base, were both from Paris. They even went to the extent of making the base out of the same stone as that used to erect the famous Arch of Triumph in the French capital.

SAMUEL DE CHAMPLAIN OR MICHEL PARTICELLI D'EMERY?

In this bronze statue Champlain looks very much like the man of action that one would expect, with pronounced cheekbones and determined features. The face, nevertheless, is one of a number of false portraits that are based on the image of a plump finance minister.

This portrait of Samuel de Champlain (right) is often used to illustrate our history books. The other engraving (below) is a depiction of Michel Particelli d'Emery. Why are they so similar? In the 19th century, when historians were writing the history of New France and of Canada, they realized that they couldn't find portraits of many of the most important figures from our history. A man was sent to Paris to look for portraits of these people. Unfortunately he wasn't able to find an image of Samuel de Champlain. But he was able to find the portrait of this man: Michel Particelli, a finance minister in the court of Louis XIII and Louis XIV – and he thought that the face looked appropriate!

A few changes were made: the hat was removed; the curtain in the background was kept. Some people seem to think that the eyes of Samuel de Champlain look a little more honest than those of Michel Particelli, but I will leave that up to the reader's judgement. The view of a European garden was replaced by a view of Quebec, seen in the distance. And so a very unpopular finance minister, accused by many of corruption, became the great hero Samuel de Champlain. To this day, most people still believe that this is Champlain's true face.

As with similar monuments made in Paris at the time, Paul Chevré's statue of the great hero dominates the composition, while allegorical figures have been placed at the base (*left*).

The angel of fame (*below*) is depicted blowing a trumpet announcing the arrival of the founder of Quebec. Beside her, a woman is writing the words of Champlain, dedicating his explorations to God. Notice the shape of her crown (*above*); it resembles a fortress. She is Quebec, the fortified city. The baby with wings, or cherub, sitting on the prow of a ship is the spirit of navigation.

PLACE D'ARMES

A MILITARY SQUARE

The Place d'Armes is one of the most important public squares in the Old City. With its park benches surrounding a central fountain erected in memory of the Récollet friars, and the presence of numerous street performers in the summer, it is one of the most animated public spaces in the upper town. Today tourist buses gather where soldiers were once marshalled to defend the walls of Quebec.

The square has always been surrounded by some of the most prominent buildings in the city. During the French Regime, these included the governor's residence, called the Chateau Saint-Louis, and the Récollet Monastery. Today, looking down from the Chateau Frontenac Hotel, we see, from left to right: the Ministry of Finance, originally built as the Provincial Courthouse in 1883-87 to replace the previous courthouse, which had been destroyed in a fire, the Anglican Cathedral of the Holy Trinity, 1800-04, and the Price Building, a small skyscraper dating from 1929. The large white building with chimneys, to the right, was the grandest hotel in the city during the early 19th century – the Union Hotel. The building now houses a tourist information bureau. All of these impressive buildings have green copper roofs. Mined in Quebec, copper is a very prestigious and durable roofing material. A copper roof can last 80 and even 100 years, so it is a perfect material to use if you know that you will own a building for a long period of time.

1 FORT SAINT-LOUIS
2 PLACE D'ARMES
3 SAINT- LOUIS STREET
4 SAINT-ANNE STREET
5 MONT- CARMEL STREET
6 PROPOSED FORTIFICATION WALL

grand fleuve de S.t Laurens

In the 1640s, Champlain's successor, Governor Huault de Montmagny, laid out the Place d'Armes, or "Military Square," beside the Fort Saint-Louis. Governor Montmagny had been given the mandate to transform the little trading post of Quebec into a town. The organizational principles established by Montmagny for the upper town and lower town remain visible in some of the city's main streets and public spaces today.

A RADIAL PLAN

This map from 1664 (*preceding page*) makes clear how these principles worked. The Old City is on a rocky point jutting out into the water. High cliffs face the St. Lawrence River, (at the bottom of the map). Facing the St. Charles River (on the right) are more cliffs, which are somewhat lower, but nevertheless offer a strong natural defence against an attack. It is only to the west, (upper part of the map), that there are neither cliffs nor water. On the map, engineer Jean Bourdon has drawn a fortification wall that he proposes to build in this area.

The governor's residence and fort stood where the boardwalk and part of the Chateau Frontenac are today. Beside the fort, the Place d'Armes served as a parade ground and a place for soldiers to muster before departing for their various duties or to defend the city in case of attack. To facilitate the movements of Governor Montmagny's troops, Jean Bourdon created a radial plan, which can be compared with a wagon wheel. The hub was the fort and the Military Square; the spokes were the straight streets radiating outwards towards the western side of the city. The rim is the curved wall that he was planning to build. Saint-Louis Street, in the centre, led out to the walls; Sainte-Anne Street (on the right of the square) would later be extended out to the walls of the city. Mont-Carmel Street (on the left) led to a gun battery.

We can still see the radial plan today in this aerial view (*preceding page, above*). The famous Chateau Frontenac Hotel now dominates the site.

(*top left*) A statue, symbolizing faith, crowns the Neo-gothic fountain in the centre of the Place d'Armes. The Monument of the Faith was erected in 1916 to commemorate the 300th anniversary of the arrival of the Récollet friars in 1615.

(center left) View of the Place d'Armes engraved from a drawing made by Richard Short after the city was conquered in 1759. The Récollet church and monastery are on the left. British soldiers are marching in the square. The effects of the recent British bombardment are visible in the background. Roofs are missing and in many cases only the stone walls remain standing. The ruins of Notre-Dame Cathedral are clearly visible behind the houses. A comparison of this 18th century view with a recent photograph (above) shows that the Bédard residence, the large grey house located to the left of the houses with the red roofs, remains almost unchanged today.

(lower left) View of the Place d'Armes by James Smillie, about 1826. After the monastery burned in 1796, two important buildings were constructed by the British authorities on the former Récollet property: the Anglican Cathedral of the Holy Trinity, built between 1800 and 1804, and the Courthouse, constructed from 1799 to 1804.

CHATEAU FRONTENAC

ICON FOR A NATION

When the Chateau Frontenac Hotel first opened its doors in 1893, this great edifice immediately became the symbol of Quebec City. But the magnificent, castle-like hotel was destined to become much more than a local landmark. As the jewel in the crown of the Canadian Pacific Railway's luxury travel empire, the Chateau Frontenac quickly became an icon for the entire nation. With its dramatic silhouette, perched high on the cliff of Cap-aux-Diamants, the Chateau Frontenac, now under the Fairmount banner, is said to be the most photographed hotel in the world.

A CASTLE ON A CLIFF

The driving force behind the construction of this magnificent building was the president of the Canadian Pacific Railway, William Cornelius Van Horne. Van Horne and his partners, who established a private company to undertake this ambitious project, would later sell the building to the CPR.

Van Horne hired American architect Bruce Price to build this great castle on a cliff. Architects in the late 19th century tended to emphasize the silhouettes of buildings and this was a certainly a great opportunity for Price. He took his inspiration from the chateaux of the Loire Valley in France and from Scottish Baronial architecture to design a romantic structure with round towers and cone-shaped roofs. Well-known for the grand residences he had built in the New York City area, Price had also designed railway cars and important buildings for the CPR, such as Windsor Station, in Montreal, and the first version of the Banff Springs Hotel, which he had constructed in wood, in Alberta. The Banff Springs Hotel exhibited characteristics of what was to come to be known as the "Chateau Style," but the Chateau Frontenac was the first hotel of this type that Price designed in brick and stone. The celebrated CPR hotel in Quebec City soon became a model for other railway hotels that were built across the country. With its impressive steep copper roofs, the "Chateau Style" inspired the design of train stations and even federal government buildings. The design of the Chateau Frontenac thus influenced architecture in Canada, from sea to sea.

GENERATIONS OF ARCHITECTS

The oldest part of the Chateau Frontenac is the Riverview wing, completed in 1893. Originally the hotel had a plan in the form of a horseshoe, with the open end facing the Governors' Garden. Then, in 1897, Price closed off the horseshoe with the Citadel wing. In 1908, American architect W.S. Painter completed the Mont-Carmel wing, with its tall tower capped by a glass roof. The high central tower of the hotel was built at the beginning of the 1920s by the firm of Edward and William S. Maxwell, of Montreal, as was the Saint-Louis wing, where the ballroom is located. In 1993, on the occasion of the centennial of the Chateau Frontenac, the Claude Pratte wing, by the Montreal firm Arcop, was inaugurated with spacious new rooms, a swimming pool, exercise facilities and an adjoining outdoor terrace. Although the hotel has been enlarged numerous times, over a span of many generations, each architect has respected the architectural character of the building designed by Bruce Price at the end of the 19th century.

The Chateau Frontenac shortly after the central tower was completed in the early 1920s.

CANADIAN PACIFIC ROUTES AROUND THE WORLD

AN EMPIRE THAT SPANNED THE WORLD

Trains, Hotels and Steam Ships

When the Chateau Frontenac Hotel opened in the early 1890s, the CPR had recently completed its rail line across Canada in the 1880s. While the transcontinental railway was a remarkable achievement in itself, it was actually only one stage of a much more ambitious project. Van Horne is quoted as saying "Canada is in a backwater. My objective is to put it on a highway." Right from the beginning, the CPR had always planned to create a fleet of ships on the Pacific Ocean to link Great Britain with its colonies in Asia. The ships would deliver the Royal Mail, as well as valuable products from the Far East, such as raw silk and tea. The CPR would also provide a passenger service. In the 1890s, Canadian Pacific was already offering the first around-the-world voyages.

The Golden Age Of Travel

By the early 20th century, the company also had a fleet of luxury steamships on the Atlantic. First-class passengers departed from Liverpool and crossed the ocean to Quebec, where they could stay at the elegant Chateau Frontenac. These well-to-do tourists could then travel across the country in first class rail cars, staying in one great castle-like hotel after another - including the dramatically located Banff Springs Hotel in the Rocky Mountains - finally ending their transcontinental journey at the Empress Hotel in Victoria, on the Pacific Coast. Those who had the means could then continue on by Canadian Pacific liner across the Pacific to Australia, Hong Kong, India and other destinations in the British Empire, always within the empire of Canadian Pacific. The company's brochures and posters advertised " The New Highway to the Orient" and " The World's Greatest Transportation System."The CPR was also an important agent of immigration; in addition to first-class passengers, the company's ships transported hundreds of thousands of immigrants, who disembarked at Quebec before travelling west on Canadian Pacific trains.

Architects and Craftsmen

For generations, the impressive interior of "The Chateau" - as locals refer to it - has served as a much-loved gathering place for the citizens of Quebec City. The main elements of the architecture and ornamentation of the interior of the Chateau Frontenac are the creation of Montreal architects Edward and W.S. Maxwell, who designed the central tower and other wings of the hotel between 1920 and 1924. The Maxwell broth-

ers, who were influenced by the Arts and Crafts movement, believed strongly in the benefits of a very close collaboration between the architect and highly skilled craftsmen. The Maxwell firm had a particularly fruitful collaboration with the craftsmen of the Bromsgrove Guild, whose studio in Montreal was a branch of the Bromsgrove Guild in Worcestershire, England. The Guild was renowned for the many complex and prestigious projects

that it had undertaken in the United Kingdom, including the ornate gates of Buckingham Palace. The Montreal branch, established in 1911, was made up almost entirely of artisans from Britain. During the early 1920s, all the models for the wood, iron, bronze and plaster ornamentation in the Chateau Frontenac, as well as numerous pieces of furniture made for the hotel, were the work of Bromsgrove artisans.

(*above left*) The staircase leading to the Salon Verchères is inspired by that of the Petit Trianon - the residence of Madame de Pompadour, and, later, of Marie Antoinette - at Versailles.

(*above right*) Details of fine metalwork ornamentation in the railing of another superb staircase that leads to the Rose Room.

The Champlain Dining Room

The décor of the Champlain dining room (*next page*), designed by architects William Maxwell and Gordon McLeod in 1926, evokes an aristocratic world, linking the Chateau Frontenac with the prestige and power associated with the governor's residence that formerly stood on this site.

An atmosphere of romance and heraldry was provided by Edwin Tappan Adney, who carved the numerous coats of arms in honour of illustrious figures from Quebec's past. Every French governor and intendant is represented, as are all the British governors. Each of the capitals of the many columns supporting the ornate ceiling is adorned with a different coat of arms. Artist James Cocker painted the richly decorated ceiling with emblems of France – the fleur-de-lis and the griffin – and of England – the lion and the rose.

The magnificent oak and marble fireplace is richly ornamented (*right, above*). Carved in oak on the hearth canopy are the French crown, Champlain's ship – the *Don de Dieu* – and the coats of arms of great men from the history of New France. From left to right: explorer Jacques Cartier, the first European to come to the site of Quebec in 1535; Pierre Dugua de Mons, in whose employ Champlain founded Quebec in 1608; Charles Huault de Montmagny, who became Quebec's first governor in 1635, and the flamboyant Cavelier de La Salle, explorer of the Mississippi and founder of Detroit.

The salamander (*right, below*) is the emblem of François I, who was King of France when Jacques Cartier first explored Canada in the 1530s and 1540s.

A ROOM WITH A VIEW

From the elegant interior of the Chateau Frontenac, visitors can enjoy a seemingly endless array of spectacular and unusual views of the city and the river.

(above) Looking west towards the fortification walls. Beyond the former Courthouse, in the right foreground, can be seen the Ursuline Convent, with its old stone buildings, inner courtyard and walled garden. To the left of the Chateau Frontenac is the Governors' Garden. On higher ground, to the far left, the Citadel dominates the city. In the far distance, past the limits of the historic district, are the Parliament building, office towers and hotels.

(far left) Looking down from the central tower over the roofs of the Riverview wing to the Dufferin Terrace, the Lower Town and the St. Lawrence River.

(left) The Champlain monument, seen from the Champlain dining room.

(right) The coat of arms of Governor Frontenac. One of the stained glass windows in the Jacques Cartier room, which display images illustrating the history of Quebec.

The Quebec Conferences of 1943 and 1944 – From left to right: The Governor General of Canada, Major General, The Earl of Athlone; The President of the United States, Franklin Delano Roosevelt; The Prime Minister of Great Britain, Sir Winston Churchill; The Prime Minister of Canada, William Lyon Mackenzie King.

Visiting Dignitaries and Historic Meetings

Decade after decade, this prestigious hotel has hosted visiting dignitaries, providing an elegant environment to receive royalty, heads of state and international meetings of historic importance.

Without a doubt, the most momentous meetings ever to take place in the Chateau Frontenac were the Quebec Conferences, held in 1943 and 1944, when British Prime Minister Winston Churchill and American President Franklin Delano Roosevelt – hosted by Canadian Prime Minister William Lyon Mackenzie King – met at Quebec to plan their strategies during World War II. While the leaders stayed in the nearby Citadel, where some of the most secret discussions took place, many meetings, as well as grand receptions and dinners, were held at the Chateau Frontenac. During these important conferences, the hotel was closed to regular customers so that it could house all the Allied officers and diplomatic personnel. Anti-aircraft guns were set up beside the Dufferin Terrace to defend the site from possible enemy attack.

DUFFERIN TERRACE

PROMENADE PAR EXCELLENCE

The Dufferin Terrace, a magnificent board-walk overlooking the lower town and the St. Lawrence River, is one of the finest urban spaces in North America. With inspiring views of the city and the countryside around Quebec, it is an ideal place to stroll, converse and enjoy entertainment by street performers.

THE GOVERNOR'S RESIDENCE

The Dufferin Terrace is located on one of the most prestigious locations in the city, the site of the Chateau Saint-Louis, which was the governor's residence for over 200 years. One of the most agreeable features of the Chateau Saint-Louis was an open platform overlooking the St. Lawrence. The view from this privileged location was reserved for the governors and their guests.

THE SITE IS OPENED TO THE PUBLIC

After the residence was destroyed by fire in 1834, Governor General Lord Durham decided that the ruins of the Chateau Saint-Louis should be covered over and a new larger platform constructed. The general public would then be able to enjoy the exceptional view of the St. Lawrence and the surrounding countryside afforded by this site at the top of the cliff. The Durham Terrace, created in 1838, was much shorter than the present board-walk. It only extended along part of the length of the present site of the Chateau Frontenac Hotel. It proved extremely popular and was lengthened in 1854 so that more people could enjoy the site. The terrace was extended to its present length in 1878-79 and renamed the Dufferin Terrace, in honour of Lord Dufferin, who had led a campaign to preserve the fortification walls of Quebec and modify them to create a promenade from which vistas of the city and surrounding area could be enjoyed.

ROSE, THISTLE, SHAMROCK AND MAPLE LEAF

A close look at the cast-iron fence of the terrace reveals the symbols of four peoples: the rose for the English, the thistle for the Scots, the shamrock for the Irish and the maple leaf for the French Canadians. Like the name canadien, *which has its origins in the early days of New France, the maple leaf was originally associated with French Canada. The maple leaf became a very popular symbol of the French Canadian people in the 1830s. However, in the later part of the 19th century, it was gradually supplanted as an emblem of French Canada by the royal fleur-de-lis of France, as the maple leaf came to be adopted as a symbol of Canada as a whole, including both its English and its French-speaking populations. The ornamentation seen in the upper portion of this detail includes elements that are reminiscent of the fleur-de-lis. All these symbols, combined together, are an expression of the complex identity of Canada – a nation of immigrants – in the 19th century.*

Chateau Saint-Louis and Fort Saint-Louis

●

The fortified habitation that Champlain had constructed close to the shore of the St. Lawrence in 1608 was ideally situated for transportation by water and for the fur trade, but the location did not take full advantage of the site's potential from a defensive point of view. So, in 1620, Champlain built a wooden fort and a residence at the top of the cliff, a location from which he and his men could more easily survey the surrounding area and defend themselves in case of attack.

While Champlain's wooden fort was gradually replaced by a more permanent structure made of stone, Governor Huault de Montmagny built a new residence, the Chateau Saint-Louis, in 1647. In 1694, Governor Frontenac had the Chateau Saint-Louis rebuilt on a somewhat grander scale to make it more worthy of the official residence of the governor of New France. In 1724, military engineer Chaussegros de Léry drew up a plan showing the enlargement of the residence that he had recently completed for Governor de Vaudreuil. The Chateau Saint-Louis would remain a seat of power for 110 more years, first for the French governors, and then for the governors of British North America. After being enlarged and transformed once more by the British for Governor Craig in 1808-11, the residence was destroyed by a fire in 1834. In all, 32 governors general had lived within the Fort Saint-Louis complex during the French and British colonial regimes.

ARCHAEOLOGICAL REMAINS

Parks Canada undertook an extensive archaeological dig on the site of the governor's residence from 2005 to 2007 (*top right*), uncovering vestiges of Fort Saint-Louis and the Chateau Saint-Louis, both of which had been rebuilt and modified over the centuries. Surviving elements of four forts and two governors' residences were revealed. Archaeologists found this early 18th century French wine bottle (*preceding page*) on the site of a latrine that had been demolished in 1720.

AN 18TH CENTURY KITCHEN

In 2008, on the occasion of Quebec City's 400th anniversary, the archaeological site was opened to the public so that visitors could walk among the ruins. Here, a guide in period costume describes the kitchen (*center right*). The fireplace is thought to date from the French period, but was probably modified by the British during major transformations that they made to the residence in 1808-11.

AN ICEHOUSE DATING FROM 1771

Earlier archaeological digs, carried out from 1980 to 1986, uncovered the remains of secondary buildings that had been part of the Chateau Saint-Louis complex. One of the most interesting structures found by the Parks Canada archaeologists was an icehouse dating from 1771 (*lower right*). A cavity had been cut out of the rock of the cliff and lined with stone, with grooves to enable a layer of wood to be added for insulation. When the structure was in use in the 18th and 19th centuries, ice – cut from the St. Lawrence – was placed in this cavity where it would remain cold for many months. Food was kept in a small building that had been constructed over the cavity and covered with a layer of earth for insulation from the summer heat. Perishable foods could be preserved in this cold room and the ice stored inside made it possible to enjoy the luxury of freezing cold drinks and desserts throughout the year. As the ice in the cavity below gradually melted, the water would have trickled down between the wooden beams at the base of the icehouse into a drain, which was also uncovered by the archaeologists.

Most of the cannons on display here were brought to Quebec by the British for the city's defence in the late 18th century and early 19th century. These are all British 32-pounders, with the exception of two cannons, which – though they look very similar – are actually Russian.

CANNONS
TROPHIES OF WAR

CAPTURED RUSSIAN CANNONS

Instead of the crown of George III (*next page, upper left*), which marks the other cannons, this weapon (*next page, upper right*) displays the coat of arms of the imperial Romanov family of Russia: a double-headed crowned eagle, with one head looking east and the other west. Written on one side of the cannon is a text in Russian, and on the other is the date when it was made, 1799. What are these cannons doing in Quebec City? We believe that they were brought here as trophies by the British, who had captured them from the Russians during the Crimean War, during the 1850s, probably at Sebastapol. Other Russian cannons are displayed elsewhere in Canada. For example, two can be seen in Montreal's Dorchester Square.

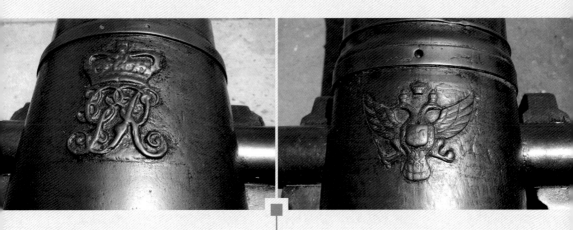

SYMBOLS OF VICTORY

The symbolic value of captured enemy cannons was very important. The British melted down Russian cannons to make the Victoria Cross, the medal awarded as the highest distinction for valour in the British Empire. Another interesting example of this phenomenon can be seen on Nelson's Column, in Trafalgar Square, in London. At the base of the column are relief sculptures depicting Nelson fighting key battles in his career. Those sculptures were made with gunmetal from captured French cannons. More war trophies in Quebec City can be seen in the National Battlefields Park, where German cannons - captured by the Canadian Army during World War I - are on display.

It is interesting to note that the Russian cannon fits perfectly onto a British gun carriage, which is clearly identified as British government property by the symbol of the broad arrow inscribed in the metal. How is it that the Russian and British artillery pieces are so compatible? Most of the British cannons in Quebec City were made at the famous Carron Foundry in Scotland. The greatest of all British cannon makers was the manager of that foundry, Charles Gascoigne. During the 1770s, due to an agreement between the British government and the Russian Empress, Catherine the Great, the Carron Foundry provided machinery and manpower to help the Russians improve their cannon production. The Russians placed large orders for cannons from the Carron firm and, on more than one occasion, staff from the Scottish foundry travelled to Russia. In 1786, Gascoigne himself sailed to Russia, with the permission of his partners. However, he never returned. Deeply in debt, and faced with personal bankruptcy at home, he accepted an offer to remain in Russia. Gascoigne caused considerable concern among the British authorities as he spent 20 years improving the Russian foundries and cannon works. Greatly honoured by Catherine the Great, he rose to the high office of State Councillor, under the Russian name of Karl Karlovich Gaskoin. His name is inscribed on the side of the Russian cannon.

"A LOOSE CANNON"

Notice the loop on the back of a British cannon (*below*). A hemp rope, running through this loop, was used to help restrain the powerful recoil when this cannon was fired. These cannons had a maximum range of approximately 2000 yards (almost 2 km). Ropes were also used to keep cannons from rolling around the decks of ships when they were not in use. Without these ropes, the heavy cannons would have been very dangerous. If, during a battle, a cannon began to roll around the decks due to the motion of heavy waves, it could crush anything in its way. You definitely wanted to avoid having "a loose

cannon" on board. That is the origin of the expression that we use in our daily speech.

GOVERNORS' GARDEN

A GREEN SPACE IN THE CITY

The site of the Governors' Garden has been a green space since the very early days of Quebec City, when Governor Charles Huault de Montmagny established his private garden here in the 1640s. Arranged in the French manner, with garden beds planted in symmetrical order, it was a pleasant place for the governor and his guests to walk; but this private walled garden also had a practical purpose, providing vegetables, herbs and fruit for meals prepared in the kitchen of the Chateau Saint-Louis.

FROM GOVERNORS' GARDEN TO PUBLIC PARK

After the conquest of 1759, it became the garden of the English governors. A watercolour painted around 1830 (*above*) by British officer James Pattison Cockburn shows that a road – today's Rue des Carrières – separated the upper garden from a lower garden, which continued down the hill below the present location of the Dufferin Terrace to the edge of the cliff. In Cockburn's illustration, two sentries guard the gate of the upper part of the garden, just in front of the Wolfe-Montcalm Monument. After the governor's residence was destroyed by fire in 1834, the garden was opened to the general public. A rather modest public park today, it is maintained by Parks Canada.

THE WOLFE-MONTCALM MONUMENT

This monument, in the form of an obelisk, was erected during the 1820s in memory of James Wolfe (the major general in charge of the British army) and the Marquis de Montcalm (the lieutenant general in charge of the French army), who both died as a result of the wounds they received during the famous Battle of the Plains of Abraham, when Quebec was conquered by the British in 1759. The creation of the monument was an initiative of Lord Dalhousie, the Governor-in-Chief of Upper and Lower Canada.

AN OBELISK

In the 19th century, obelisks were often used for monuments having funerary associations. Other examples are the Washington Monument, in Washington DC, and the obelisk in centre of the Place de la Concorde in Paris, which was erected on the site where Louis XVI and many of the aristocrats of France were guillotined during the French Revolution. While the monument in Paris is an ancient Egyptian obelisk, with a history going back thousands of years, the obelisk in Quebec City was designed by a British officer in 1827 and is made of local limestone.

The Wolfe-Montcalm Monument bears an inscription in Latin that could be roughly translated as:

Courage gave them a common death
History, a common fame
Posterity, a common monument

It is said to be the only monument that honours both the victor and the vanquished.

THE LAST VETERAN

When the first stone of the obelisk was laid during an impressive ceremony on November 20, 1827, the last veteran of the Battle of the Plains of Abraham, James Thompson, was in attendance. Considering that the battle took place in 1759, one could say that he was "getting on" by this time. In fact, he died three years later, at the age of 98.

In his youth, this Scotsman had been a giant of a man, known for his great physical strength. He fought during the capture of Louisbourg in 1758, as well as participating in the siege of Quebec in 1759. In 1775, he helped to fight off American revolutionaries laying siege to the city. He then worked for many years

as overseer of works for the British Army and was responsible for improvements to the fortifications of Quebec in the late 18th and early 19th centuries.

During the long ceremony of the laying of the first stone, the aged veteran was supported by the arm of Captain John Crawford Young, the officer of the 79th Regiment who had designed the monument. As the last surviving veteran of the battle – and as a highly respected member of the Masonic Order – James Thompson was given the honour of tapping the monument three times with the Mystic Masonic Hammer. It was the last time the old gentleman was seen in public.

Looking down on the Governors' Garden from the Chateau Frontenac. Beyond the residential streets of the upper town can be seen the great star-shaped fortress of the Citadel of Quebec, built by the British Military between 1820 and 1831.

MAISON JACQUET

THE OLDEST HOUSE IN QUEBEC CITY

Now occupied by a restaurant, the *Maison Jacquet* is the oldest surviving house in the city of Quebec. The original dwelling, which can be seen on the right-hand side of the building, was constructed in 1675 and enlarged in 1699. The very sharp angle of its steep gable roof is typical of the period. An addition, located on the left side, dates from approximately 1820. The roof of this part of the building has a shallower profile, as was customary during the 19th century.

KEEPING WARM

The Jacquet house, with its whitewashed stone walls, gives us a good idea of what many houses in the upper town looked like in the 17th and 18th centuries. Although it was one the largest houses on Saint-Louis Street at that time, it now appears quite small when compared with the 19th and 20th century buildings that surround it (*above right*). This has partly to do with improved methods of heating and insulation, as succeeding generations of builders managed to better adapt Quebec houses to the city's severe winters. At first, people had tried to keep warm using open fireplaces, like those they had in France, but this kind of heating method was not adequate in the cold climate of Quebec. With the introduction of efficient iron stoves and other improvements in the 18th century, it became much easier to keep large interior spaces relatively comfortable during the colder months of the year.

A CRAFTSMAN'S HOME

During the late 17th and early 18th centuries, the Jacquet house was the home of some of Quebec's most successful builders and craftsmen, including Pierre-Noël Levasseur, the artist who sculpted the ornamentation of the Ursuline Chapel.

URSULINE CONVENT

A GIRLS SCHOOL SINCE 1639

One of the oldest institutions in Quebec, the Ursuline Convent continues today in the educational role for which it was first established, housing one of the finest girls' schools in the city. The Ursuline nuns, who came to Quebec in 1639 to educate Amerindian girls and French girls in the settlement, established their convent and school on this site in the upper town in 1642.

Cloistered until the 1960s, Ursuline nuns took vows to devote their lives to God and to have little or no contact with the outside world once they entered the convent. If friends or relatives came to visit a nun, they were taken to a special room called the "parloir" (from the French word *parler*, "to speak"), where they could speak to her through a metal grill. The sisters constructed their buildings around an enclosed courtyard so that they could go outdoors and get fresh air without seeing anyone from outside the convent.

A courtyard of the Ursuline Convent (*preceding page, foreground*) serves as a play area for girls attending the school. The courtyard is bounded by the Interior Chapel and other wings, which were constructed in stages over four centuries. Behind these buildings, to the far-right, is the most recent construction: the Marie-Guyart wing, inaugurated in 1989. While retaining the traditional steep roof and stone construction, this late 20th century structure has a very modern interior which includes two gymnasiums.

The two buildings which make up the Ursuline Chapel (*above*) can be seen in this bird's-eye view. The External Chapel, with a statue of Saint Joseph over the entrance, and the Interior Chapel, with its domed roof, are arranged in an L-shaped plan.

(*above*) Bronze sculpture by Emile Brunet, 1942, depicting Marie de l'Incarnation, who founded the Ursuline Convent and school in 1639, with a Huron girl and a French girl. A source of spiritual inspiration for generations of Ursuline nuns and their students, Marie de l'Incarnation – who was beatified in 1980 – was also a remarkable intellectual and artist. In addition to translating sacred texts into Iroquois and Algonquian, and creating dictionaries of the native languages, she wrote thousands of letters to France describing life in the convent and the colony. A highly skilled embroiderer, she played an important role in establishing the sacred arts in the convent. (*below*) View across the playground towards the Interior Chapel (1901-02) On the left-hand side is the Sainte-Famille wing (1686). Rising high above the roofs of the convent is the Price Building, dating from 1929.

The garden of the Ursuline Convent is a secret, hidden corner of the Old City. In the past, the upper town was filled with gardens. One of the streets that borders the Ursuline property is Des Jardins Street, (or garden street). Three religious institutions that were founded in the 17th century - the Ursuline Convent, the Récollet Monastery and the Jesuit College - all once had gardens along this street. Some upper town gardens, like that of the Ursulines, have survived, in part at least, until the present day, but are hidden by the high walls and houses that surround them, so that most passers-by never suspect their existence.

The Ursuline Chapel

The Ursuline Chapel is divided into two parts: an External Chapel, which is open to the general public, and an Interior Chapel, which is reserved for the nuns and the girls who attend their school. The two places of worship, separated by a metal grill, share the same sanctuary area, and the pulpit is placed in such a way that the priest could address both groups without either seeing the other. Both

chapels were reconstructed at the beginning of the 20th century, but the original ornamentation of the External Chapel, sculpted by Pierre-Noël Levasseur between 1726 and 1736, was retained. In the colonial context of the early 18th century, the exteriors of chapels and churches tended to be very simple. It would have been too expensive to create an elaborate stone façade, and an ornate wooden façade would not have stood up well to the severe climatic conditions here. The exteriors of religious buildings were thus kept quite plain, with stone whitewashed walls and a few niches to hold statues. Almost all the emphasis was placed on the interior and, especially, the retable – the impressive ornamental ensemble behind the main altar.

THE RETABLE

The retable of the Ursuline Chapel (*preceding page*), is divided into three parts by columns, somewhat like a triumphal arch. It might be thought of as a symbolic gate to heaven. At the highest level, in a place of honour, Saint Joseph is shown holding the Christ Child. There was a particular devotion to Saint Joseph, patron saint of New France, at the Ursuline convent. The painting above the altar depicts the Nativity. The Holy Family was always revered with a special devotion in the French colony. To the right is a statue of Saint Ursula, patron saint of the Ursuline Nuns, and to the left, with his bishop's mitre, is Saint Augustine. It was Saint Augustine who wrote the rules followed by the Ursulines and many other religious orders.

Saint Augustine (*below, left*) is shown holding a flaming heart, signifying that he preached the love of God. Saint Ursula (*below, right*) is shown holding her attributes: an arrow, because she is said to have been killed with arrows for refusing to marry Attila the Hun, and a palm branch, a symbol of her martyrdom.

The Ursulines did magnificent gold leaf work to enhance the sculptures and ornamentation in their chapel. Before the gold leaf was applied, elaborate low-relief work was added by the nuns to the clothing of the statues to create the appearance of richly embroidered fabric. The Ursuline nuns, who had brought knowledge of the sacred arts with them from France, were specialists in the application of gold leaf and provided income for their convent by gilding sculptures and ornamentation for other churches in New France.

Viewed together, the carved panels (*above*) on the two doors illustrate the story of the Annunciation, when the angel Gabriel announced to the Virgin Mary that she would be the mother of Christ. On one panel, the angel Gabriel descends on a cloud. On the other, the Virgin Mary kneels in prayer. She looks up towards a dove, representing the Holy Spirit. On the pedestals beneath each of the retable's columns are low-relief sculptural panels (*below*) that depict different saints, along with their attributes. From left to right: Saint John the Evangelist, whose attribute is the eagle, Saint Peter, who holds the keys to the gates of heaven, Saint Paul, whose symbol is the sword, and Saint John the Baptist, who is identified by the animal skin he wears and the lamb at his feet.

THE RETABLE OF THE SACRED HEART

Facing the Interior Chapel is the retable of the Sacred Heart. The angels sitting above the cornice hold a cartouche (*right*) on which instruments of the Passion are depicted – these are objects associated with Christ's crucifixion, including the whip that was used to lash him, the lance that pierced his side and the ladder which was used to take him down from the cross.

ART SAVED FROM THE FRENCH REVOLUTION

The painting over the main altar (*see pages 60-61*), depicting Joseph, Mary and the baby Jesus, surrounded by adoring shepherds, may have been in the collection of the Jesuits before it came to the Ursuline Convent. For many years, this work was attributed to Charles Le Brun, the great painter of the court of Louis XIV. Today, however, credit for the painting is given to an "artist unknown."

While the painting of the Holy Family is thought to have come from the Jesuit College, other fine works in the Ursuline Chapel, such as the superb painting of Jesus at the Table of the Simon the Pharisee (located over the entrance door), came to Quebec from France after the French

Revolution. Amid the violence and destruction of the Revolution, many works of art from religious institutions were confiscated and ended up being purchased by speculators. Among the refugees who fled the Revolution were two priests from Paris, the Desjardins brothers, who arrived in Quebec in the 1790s. Philippe Jean-Louis Desjardins later returned to Paris, where he purchased two large collections of paintings and sent them to his brother, Louis-Joseph, in Quebec. Abbé Louis-Joseph Desjardins, who was chaplain to the Augustinian nuns and spiritual advisor to the Ursulines, arranged for the works to be displayed in the convents and sold to religious institutions.

An angel blows a trumpet atop the elaborate sounding board of the pulpit.

· 63

The Interior Chapel

The Interior Chapel (*left*), reserved for the nuns and the girls attending the school, dates from 1901. The architect, David Ouellet, also reconstructed the External Chapel, used by the general public, the following year. While he had to make the new version of the External Chapel relatively simple, so as not to distract from the early 18th century ornamentation by Pierre-Noël Levasseur, he had a freer hand in the Interior Chapel, where he took inspiration from Romano-Byzantine architecture. With robust mouldings and a domed ceiling, the Interior Chapel is very impressive. Throne-like chairs, called stalls (*above*), are positioned on either side of the chapel, enabling the nuns to sing alternate verses back and forth to each other during the divine office. Every stall has a small kneeling stool, which pivots outward, so that the nuns can turn to pray before the Altar of the Sacred Heart

THE SACRED ARTS

The Ursuline nuns did splendid embroidery work in fine silk, silver and gold thread. Detail of the Nativity altar frontal, created by the workshop of the Ursuline Convent of Quebec during the second half of the 17th century. The convent museum possesses a remarkable collection of embroideries, sacred art and objects from the daily life of the convent and school over the centuries.

A LIVING HISTORY

While the Ursuline Chapel and Museum are open to the public, access to the interior of the other historic buildings of the convent is a rare privilege.

An ancient stone sink, set in a wall of the Intercommunity Room (upper left), and a fireplace holding a collection of British cannon balls that landed in the convent during the siege of 1759. In the vaulted basements of the Ursuline convent, a well (upper right) dating from the 17th century stands next to a massive fireplace from the same period. Fine 17th century panelling in the Intercommunity Room (lower left). A corridor in the convent (lower right), with an iron fire door surmounted by a statue of Our Lady of the Angels. The Saint Augustine staircase (next page) has been part of the life of the convent and girls' school since 1689.

STREET PATTERNS

IT ALL BEGAN WITH A STREAM...

Donnacona and Du Parloir streets form an irregular shape as they skirt the edge of the Ursuline property – with one large curve in front of the main entrance of the convent, followed by another curve as Donnacona turns to join Des Jardins Street. A map dating from 1685 (*preceding page*) shows that a stream once followed exactly this course. The shape of the stream determined the shape of the streets, as well as property boundaries on either side. As a result, some of the houses are rather oddly shaped indeed.

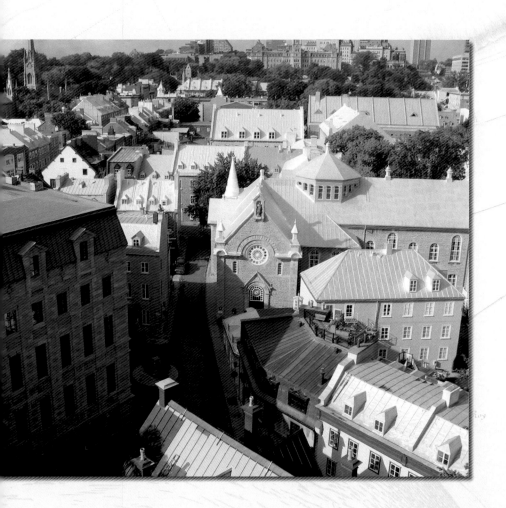

IRREGULAR STREETS AND ODDLY SHAPED BUILDINGS

One of the houses has a very narrow façade, although it is actually larger than it might first appear because it opens up into a wedge shape behind. The house next door has an unusual shape as well, with one wall joining the façade of the narrow house at a very sharp angle and its other wall curving around the corner as it follows the path of the former stream bed (*left, below*). This is a good example of how, in older cities, the irregular shapes of streets and sometimes buildings can often be traced back to natural obstacles that had to be avoided. Elsewhere in North America, we can think of the city of Boston, where some of the earliest streets are said to have begun as cow paths. Perhaps the cows were avoiding natural obstacles as the people of Quebec avoided this stream.

WHY QUEBEC FEELS LIKE SUCH AN ANCIENT CITY

While most of the surviving buildings in the historic district date from the 19th century, visitors often remark that Quebec, with its narrow winding streets, has the feeling of much older cities in Europe. Quebec City does, in fact, share certain basic characteristics with ancient cities of the past. When choosing a site, the founders of these cities usually sought a promontory, a high place that would be easy to defend. Often these high, rocky places had a rather uneven topography, so that the streets had to be adapted to the irregular features of the landscape. Those seeking an ideal location for a settlement also almost always sought to locate it beside a body of water. This was crucial for transportation and trade in past centuries, when roads were usually either very poor, or non-existent. Thus, in historic cities we often find a lower town and an upper town, as in Quebec City, with a commercial area by the water and a fortified area above.

CATHEDRAL OF THE HOLY TRINITY

ENGLISH ARCHITECTURE IN A COLONIAL CONTEXT

The Cathedral of the Holy Trinity, constructed between 1800 and 1804, was the first Anglican Cathedral to be built outside the British Isles. The British had, of course, built many churches in their colonies prior to this, but they had never constructed a cathedral, the principal church of a diocese where the bishop has his throne.

DESIGNED BY BRITISH MILITARY OFFICERS

The military officers who designed the Cathedral of the Holy Trinity, Captain William Hall and Major William Robe, were very proud of what they had done, and Major Robe wrote a detailed text describing how they had devised and built the church.

SAINT MARTIN-IN-THE-FIELDS

They took inspiration from the architecture of a famous London church, Saint Martin-in-the-Fields. If you are familiar with that church on Trafalgar Square, you will realise that the façade of Holy Trinity is much simpler. Saint Martin-in-the-Fields has an impressive portico, with large columns. Here in Quebec City, due to the state of the quarries at the time, it was not possible to extract

stones that were large enough to make such columns at a reasonable price. Instead, flat columns, called pilasters, were placed against the façade.

DEALING WITH A WINTER CLIMATE

The shape of the pediment - the triangular form beneath the roofline of the Cathedral - is rather unusual, Its proportions do not follow the strict rules of classical architecture; the slopes are far too high and steep. The interesting thing is that, originally, the pediment did have the right shape. However, there was so much trouble with snow accumulation and water infiltration that those responsible for the church decided to follow the local French tradition and build a higher, steeper roof to replace the first one. The stone walls in the front and back were raised to meet the new roof. If you could go inside the attic of this church, you would see that the original line of the first pediment is still visible. Holy Trinity is an excellent example of how colonial architecture often had to be adapted to local conditions; a great model from London was simplified for financial reasons - and for lack of the right materials - and then transformed once more because of the severe climatic conditions here.

SUPERB PROPORTIONS

The proportions of the interior of the church are superb. Colonial architecture sometimes has a certain awkwardness in the overall design. Locally trained builders and amateur architects might be able to copy the form of the capital of an Ionic column correctly from a pattern book, but they often had difficulty combining all the elements into a coherent, well-proportioned architectural composition. In this case, however, the British officers who designed the Cathedral truly had a sophisticated understanding of the principles of classical architecture – to the extent that one could place a perfect sphere in the sanctuary area. This is why one feels a sense of harmony when one enters the church – the proportions are just right.

It is hard to imagine military officers designing such a church today. Officers in the late 18th and early 19th centuries received a very different kind of education. These British officers, who were trained at the Royal Military Academy at Woolwich, were taught surveying, map making and topographical drawing. Many became skilled draughtsmen. The officers, who almost always came from an aristocratic background, had a lot of free time to pursue personal interests when they were not at war. Some became talented amateur watercolour painters who recorded scenes and people in the countries where they were stationed. Others became amateur architects. A few years after designing the Cathedral of the Holy Trinity, Major Robe was commanding the artillery in battles against the armies of Napoleon. These British officers were certainly able to turn their talents to a wide variety of tasks.

Major Robe, in his detailed plans for the interior of the church, took inspiration from the work of Italian Renaissance architects. The Ionic columns in the nave, for example, are modelled on the work of Palladio. The proportions of the columns in the east window are taken from Vignola.

The Crown paid for construction of the church, and King George III gave magnificent silver (see pages 80-81) to this first Anglican Cathedral built outside the British Isles. The Royal Arms of George III (above) identify the pew that was reserved for members of the Royal Family, or their representatives, who might worship in the church. However, in today's more democratic society the Royal Pew is no longer used. When Queen Elizabeth and Prince Philip came to the Cathedral in 1987, they did not want to worship above the people, choosing instead to sit in two chairs placed in the centre aisle.

The bishop's throne (right) is associated with the memory of a great tree that once grew on the grounds of the church. This tree was so ancient that it was believed, according to oral tradition, that Samuel de Champlain had smoked the peace pipe with the native peoples under its branches. When the tree was struck by lightning in 1845, some of its wood was used to make the bishop's throne.

Music

A RARE 18th CENTURY ENGLISH CHAMBER ORGAN

The small chamber organ (*left*) beside the bishop's throne was originally made for a country house in England – Oakes Park, near Sheffield – by John England and Son of London in 1790. It was restored and installed in the Cathedral of the Holy Trinity in 2004, thanks to the generous gift of an anonymous donor, and inaugurated with a concert of period music to mark the Cathedral's 200th anniversary.

LOOKING TOWARDS THE MAIN ORGAN

The main organ (*next page*) has been replaced and rebuilt a number of times. The dark burgundy and gold colours in the decoration of the organ case date from the late 19th century, when a new organ was made by Samuel Warren of Montreal in 1884-85. The organ was then rebuilt and enlarged by Casavant in 1909; additional work was done by the British firm of Hill, Norman and Beard in 1959. During the last two rebuilds, the original Warren case and a high percentage of the existing pipes were retained.

The prayer stool in the foreground was superbly carved by the English sculptor Edmond Burton; it was designed by the prominent British architect Mervyn E. Macartney, who was an influential proponent of the Arts and Crafts movement. Through his work and publications, Macartney strove to bring architects and craftsmen to work together as equals in the creative process.

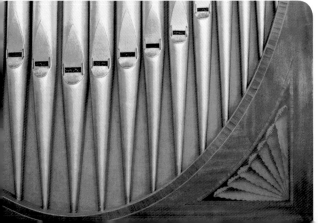

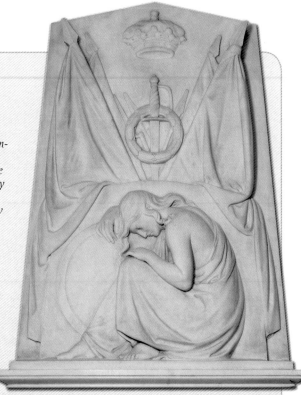

MEMORIES OF EMPIRE

It is fascinating to look at the commemorative plaques and monuments that
adorn the walls of the Cathedral of the
Holy Trinity. This French-speaking city
was once part of the British Empire,
and members of the British aristocracy
were constantly passing through here.
Government officials and officers
might be stationed in Australia,
Jamaica, Halifax or Quebec. There
is a monument (below, right) for
soldiers whose regiment fought at
Waterloo and Lucknow in India.
Another monument is in memory
of an officer who was born to an
English military family in Quebec
City and fought for the British
Empire in Afghanistan before
being killed while leading his
troops in a battle in India.

From Waterloo to Quebec
- Monument to the Duke of Richmond

This impressive monument (above, right) is in memory of the Duke of
Richmond (1764-1818). The Duke and his wife gave a famous
ball on the eve of the Battle of Waterloo, an event that was
immortalized in a poem by Lord Byron. Later, when serving
as governor-in-chief of British North America, the Duke of
Richmond was bitten by a rabid fox and died of rabies. He is
buried under the sanctuary of this church.

A Rarely noticed Masterpiece - Monument
to Thomas Dunn

Thomas Dunn (1729-1818) was
a very successful businessman,
seignior, judge and colonial
administrator. This re-
markable work (left),
which was sculpted
in London,
often goes
unnoticed
because it
is placed
high on a
wall above
the south
gallery.

Stained glass

Originally there were no stained glass windows in the Cathedral, so that one could see though clear glass to the cityscape beyond. Then, beginning in the second half of the 19th century, memorial windows were installed, given to commemorate past members of the congregation and clergy who served at the Cathedral.

Detail of the east window (*above*): Dominating the church from above the main altar, this magnificent window – dedicated to the memory of the third Bishop, George Jehoshaphat Mountain – was made in 1864 by the Clutterbuck firm of London. The intensity of the reds and blues is exceptional.

Detail of a window depicting the Nativity (*below*): This window, one of the finest in the Cathedral, is in memory of a premier of the Province of Quebec, Sir Henri-Gustave Joly de Lotbinière, and his wife Margaretta Josepha Gowen. It was made in 1910 by the firm of Clayton and Bell, in London, England.

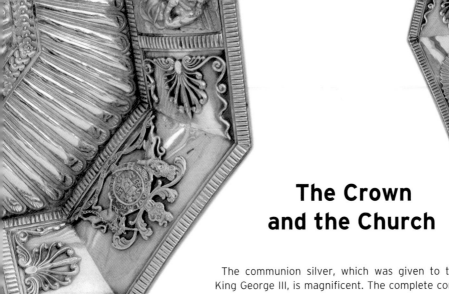

The Crown
and the Church

The communion silver, which was given to the Cathedral by King George III, is magnificent. The complete communion service was made in London by the Royal Silversmiths, Rundell & Bridge, in 1802-03. The altar candlesticks, chalices and other elements of the ten-piece service bear the arms of the King and of the Diocese of Quebec. Truly a royal gift!

The octagonal alms dish is very richly adorned. In the centre, the Last Supper is portrayed in high relief. Surrounding the Last Supper is a border with depictions of the Four Evangelists. The four corners display the arms of the Diocese of Quebec, the arms of the King and the Holy Trinity, symbolized by a circle of shining rays, a triangle and a dove.

THE ARMS OF THE DIOCESE

The coat of arms of the Diocese of Quebec (left) is displayed above the bishop's throne. At the top of the coat of arms is a bishop's mitre. The shield is divided into two parts - the upper part, red and the lower part, blue. A wavy line represents the ocean that separates Quebec from the mother country, England. The lion of England holds a key that indicates the sacred confidence of the Sovereign in the Bishop. The subordination of the Bishop of Quebec to the Archbishop of Canterbury is symbolized by the four crosses, which are taken from the Archbishop's coat of arms. The book, with the bishop's crosier, is an emblem of the gospel.

Altar candlestick (right). A close look (below) reveals the remarkable artistry of the silversmith, allowing us to appreciate details such as the very expressive rams' heads and the monogram IHS, based on the name of Christ in ancient Greek.

CITY HALL SQUARE

A CENTRE OF PUBLIC LIFE

Visitors often compare the picturesque atmosphere of Quebec's historic district with that of much older European cities. The public squares of Old Quebec contribute greatly to this European feeling. These squares have always served as centres of public life. One of the principle open spaces in the upper town, City Hall Square is bordered by some of the capital's most prominent buildings. Notre-Dame de Québec Basilica and the Old Seminary of Quebec have dominated the eastern side of this open area since the 17th century. Across the square from these religious institutions is Quebec's City Hall. It is no accident that the Basilica and the City Hall, which represent religious and civic authority, are located so that their entrance doors are positioned to face directly one another across the square.

In the centre of the square is a monument commemorating Canada's first Cardinal, Elzéar Alexandre Taschereau. His statue, looking down from a granite pedestal, embodies the prestige and authority of the Catholic Church in Quebec at the time when this monument was erected in 1923. In those days, this open space was not called City Hall Square but rather *Place de la Basilique*, or Basilica Square.

A MARKET SQUARE

Numerous shops face this public space, as they have for centuries. This open area became a centre of commercial life in the early 1600s when the upper town market was established in the square. Markets were of crucial importance for the citizens of the city, who came each week to purchase food to feed their families, hay to feed their horses and wood to heat their homes. Market

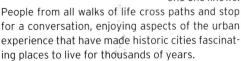

squares were established in different quarters of the city to ensure that citizens would not have to travel long distances to make their purchases. For generations, people of every social class gathered in these open spaces to interact and learn the latest news. Here the town crier made announcements, and public punishments – and sometimes executions – took place.

A PLACE TO MEET

While markets have not been held in City Hall Square since 1875, this open space in the upper town still retains characteristics of the kind of meeting place that gives so much animation and character to historic cities. City Hall Square remains an open area where those who live and work in the Old City can cross paths and meet on a daily basis. Here residents and visitors sit to read or eat their lunch, or gather in large numbers to watch street performers. In today's world, in which most urban life is dominated by the automobile, people who live and work in Quebec's historic district are still able to go about many of their daily activities on foot. One of the greatest pleasures of life in the historic district is that it is almost impossible to step outside for five minutes without bumping into someone one knows. People from all walks of life cross paths and stop for a conversation, enjoying aspects of the urban experience that have made historic cities fascinating places to live for thousands of years.

CITY HALL
SITE OF THE JESUIT COLLEGE

Quebec's City Hall, constructed in 1895-96, stands on the former site of the Jesuit College, founded in 1635. The Jesuits began the construction of their buildings on this site in 1647. On the lawn of City Hall, just to the left of the stairs leading to the entrance, is a stone with a plaque commemorating the college. The image on the plaque depicts the educational institution as it appeared after the building had been enlarged and partially reconstructed in 1725.

The engraving below, printed in London, was part of a series of images made after drawings done by British officer Richard Short after the siege of 1759. Damage from British cannon fire is visible in the walls of the building. The Jesuit Church is shown in the middle of the picture, to the left of the college. The church, which was demolished in 1807, stood approximately where a bus shelter and Des Jardins Street are located today. Prior to the construction of an underground parking lot beneath City Hall, the foundations of the Jesuit Church were uncovered by archaeologists in 1971.

ARCHAEOLOGICAL DISCOVERIES

The first archaeological dig on the site of the college was carried out in 1878. At that time, the graves of Jesuit priests were found where a Jesuit chapel had been located, to the left of the main entrance door of the college. More recently, in 1992, an archaeological dig was carried out beneath the paved walkway leading to the entrance of the City Hall. This time, the skeletons of two more Jesuit priests were found.

You never know what you may find when you dig down in an historic town like Quebec. The City has its own archaeology department, which works very effectively to ensure that a wealth of history, hidden underground, is analysed and protected.

FRENCH AND AMERICAN INFLUENCES

Quebec's City Hall, built according to the plans of architect Georges-Émile Tanguay in 1895, shows the influence of American architect Henry Hobson Richardson, with its tall, round-headed windows, and broadly curved entrance arch, supported by squat columns. While taking inspiration from an American model, Tanguay nevertheless remained loyal to French classical traditions. Rather than employ the asymmetrical massing typical of American city halls of the period, he designed the façade of his building with a central entrance pavilion flanked by projecting wings. The Quebec architect was able to add a picturesque touch, without disturbing the symmetry of the main façade, by placing a clock tower on the Fabrique Street side of the building,

SYMBOL OF THE JESUITS

In Short's illustration, a triangular pediment crowns the main doorway of the college. On the lawn of City Hall, near the commemorative plaque, the original stone pediment is on display (below). Carved in the limestone is the monogram of the Jesuits: IHS, with a cross above the H.

TASCHEREAU MONUMENT
CANADA'S FIRST CARDINAL

In the centre of City Hall Square stands a monument in memory of Archbishop Elzéar-Alexandre Taschereau, who became the first Canadian cardinal in 1886. Created in the context of an international competition, this fine work by sculptor André Vermare and architect Maxime Roisin – both from France – was inaugurated in 1923.

The bronze sculptural panels at the base of the monument depict important scenes from the Cardinal's life. One panel emphasizes his role as an educator, as director of the Seminary and rector of Laval University. The university, founded in 1852, is shown in the background. In another panel, the prelate is shown caring for the sick, at great risk to his own health, as thousands died on a quarantine island – La Grosse Île – during the typhus epidemic of 1848. In a third panel, he is shown praying beneath the great baldachino of Notre-Dame de Québec Basilica. Here the Cardinal's role in the introduction of a special religious devotion to the Blessed Sacrament is emphasized.

In 1923, this image of the baldachino must have had a very special significance for the citizens of the city. Notre-Dame de Québec Basilica had just recently been destroyed by a terrible fire in December of 1922. Both authors of the Taschereau monument were to play crucial roles in the reconstruction of the great church. Maxime Roisin was one of the principle architects, while André Vermare was chosen to re-create the extraordinary baldachino, which had originally been made by Quebec artist François Baillairgé at the end of the 18th century.

Notre-Dame de Québec

RISEN LIKE A PHOENIX FROM THE ASHES

Notre-Dame de Québec Basilica, which began as a much smaller church in the 1647, became the first Catholic Cathedral north of Mexico in 1674. Two hundred years later, Pope Pius IX honoured Notre-Dame de Québec by making it the first minor basilica in North America, thus recognizing the central role of this church in the establishment of the Catholic faith across the continent. The Bishop of Quebec once presided over a diocese that extended through all the lands claimed by New France, an area larger than Europe. With the passage of time, the original Diocese of Quebec has gradually been broken up into smaller units, so that, today, over 150 dioceses in Canada and the United States occupy this vast territory.

DESTRUCTION BY FIRE AND WAR

After being enlarged in the late 1600s and in the 1740s, Notre-Dame de Québec was almost completely destroyed by English cannon fire in 1759. The church was then rebuilt and embellished by generations of architects, artists and craftsmen, with the last major work being completed in 1920-21. On December 22, 1922, a terrible fire left the church a smoking ruin, with only the stone walls remaining. In 1923, work began yet again on the reconstruction of Notre-Dame de Québec within its original walls. The recreation of the original ornamentation - almost exactly as it had been before the fire - was a remarkable undertaking.

A CATHEDRAL AND A BASILICA

Notre-Dame de Québec Church is both a cathedral and a basilica. A Cathedral is the spiritual and administrative centre of a diocese, where the bishop has his throne. A basilica, on the other hand, is a church of significant size which has some special significance for the Catholic Church and is honoured by the Pope with this title. There are two minor basilicas in the Quebec City region: Notre-Dame de Québec and Sainte-Anne de Beaupré, a famous pilgrimage church situated on the Beaupré Coast. In 1922, both basilicas were tragically destroyed by fire and then rebuilt with much effort and at great expense.

BUILDING AND RE-BUILDING

First called Notre-Dame de la Paix, in celebration of a treaty signed with the Iroquois, the original church of 1647 had a plan in the shape of a Latin cross. When Notre-Dame became a cathedral in 1674, Bishop Laval decided to have his church enlarged and made more magnificent, to reflect its enhanced status. Despite some help from Louis XIV, Bishop Laval was obliged to simplify his project due to limited funding. A new façade for the church remained isolated out in the middle of the square for a number of years before the nave was finally extended out to meet it in 1697. From 1744 to 1748, military engineer Gaspard Chaussegros de Léry enlarged the church once more by adding

THE FACADE

side aisles, extending the sanctuary to its present length and raising the height of the nave, which he lit with clearstory windows from above. He also drew up plans for an elegant classical façade and interior ornamentation, which could be added later when funds became available. Before this could be accomplished, however, the church was destroyed by English fire bombs during the siege of 1759. Notre-Dame was reconstructed, with some modifications, by Jean Baillairgé in the 1760s. In the years to come, other members of the Baillairgé family were to play a leading role in the construction and ornamentation of this great church.

The Neo-classical façade of Notre-Dame de Québec (*above left*), which dates from 1844, is the work of architect Thomas Baillairgé. The elegant, multi-layered composition in finely cut stone was not completed as originally intended. Thomas Baillairgé's plans called for a symmetrical design with two identical towers, but construction of the north tower (left side) was stopped only part way up after a weakness was discovered in the foundations. The tower on the south side, which Baillairgé had intended to replace, thus retained its 18th century form.

At the top of the baldachino is Christ the Redeemer, surrounded by rays of light and angels. He is holding the Cross and is standing on an orb which symbolizes the world.

THE BALDACHINO

The most remarkable element of the interior of Notre-Dame de Québec is the magnificent baldachino, an impressive golden sculptural canopy, over the sanctuary area. While the original was destroyed in the fire of 1922, the present reconstruction, by Parisian sculptor André Vermare (*see pages 90-91*), corresponds quite closely to the appearance of the work completed by Francois Baillairgé in 1793.

As a very young man, François (son of Jean Baillairgé) had been sent to Paris for an academic education in the arts from 1778 to 1781. When he returned to Quebec, he had a considerable influence on the art of the colony, which had become increasingly isolated from its sources in France.

THE BAILLAIRGÉ FAMILY

After Notre-Dame was destroyed by cannon fire in 1759, reconstruction began in 1766 under the direction of Jean Baillairgé, a carpenter and wood-carver from the Poitou region of France who adapted to the needs of the colony by becoming a contractor and architect. The Baillairgé family would come to dominate the building industry in Quebec City, providing five generations of architects, artists and engineers, including Jean Baillairgé, François Baillairgé, Thomas Baillairgé and Charles Baillairgé, who all worked on Notre-Dame de Québec during the 18th and 19th centuries. The impressive cast-iron fence (page 95), with its richly ornamented entrance gates, was designed by Charles Baillairgé in 1857.

The Virgin Mary is flanked by two angels (*above*). Angels support the great carved branches of the baldachino (*preceding page*).

GOLD LEAF AND "DUTCH GOLD"

The golden ornamentation of the basilica is most impressive, In 1983, however, due to its poor state of conservation, much of the original gold leaf was replaced by a substitute for gold called "Dutch gold," which consists of thin sheets of copper with only about 2% gold content. To ensure that the copper would not oxidize and darken when exposed to the air, the Dutch gold had to be covered with a special varnish.

Fortunately, in 1984, art conservators were able to restore the true gold leaf that adorns the altar, the tabernacle and the canopy over the bishop's throne, revealing the magnificent gilding that had been done during the reconstruction after the fire of 1922.

The beauty of the contrasting polished and mat surfaces is particularly evident in this detail of the canopy over the bishop's throne (right). The face of the angel was quite fragile and had to be carefully restored to stabilize the preparatory undercoating (required before the application of the gold leaf), which had cracked over time.

THE ALTAR, TABERNACLE AND RETABLE

While not identical to the one that was destroyed in the fire, the tabernacle (*above*) - like the original - has been treated as if it were a miniature building. Its design is inspired by the architecture of Saint Peter's Church in Rome. The dome and columns (*next page, upper right*), with their polished gold surfaces, are brighter and shinier than other parts of the structure. In the finest gold leaf work there is always a distinction between those elements which project forward and those that are set back. The elements that are closer to us are given a polished surface, while those that are set back are given a mat surface. This creates an impression of depth and makes all the details more clearly visible when seen from a distance.

The architectural ornamentation of the sanctuary in the background is inspired by the original late 18th century work by François Baillairgé and his father, Jean. Thanks to his experience in Paris, François was able to introduce a renewed sophistication to church design. At Notre-Dame de

Québec, in contrast to the usual approach taken by the colony's sculptors, who made each object - retable, pulpit, or church warden's pew - as if it were a separate piece of furniture, the Baillairgés brought all the elements together in a logical, architectural composition which extends throughout the sanctuary.

Statues of saints flank the altarpiece. From left to right: Saint Joseph, whose symbol is the lily; Saint Louis, who is holding the relics he brought back from the Holy Land - the crown of thorns and nails that were believed to have been used in the Crucifixion; Saint Flavian and Saint Felicity, who were early Christian martyrs; and finally, Saint Paul, whose symbol is the sword. Saint Peter, with the keys to the gates of heaven, cannot be seen in this picture, but is shown in a separate photograph (*lower right*).

François de Laval,
First Bishop of New France

The funerary chapel of François de Laval (1623-1708) is a remarkable late 20th century work which was created by architect Émile Gilbert, with artists Jules Lasalle and Marion Ducharme, in 1993. The recumbent figure in bronze lies on a slab of black granite which has been made to look as if it has risen up from the granite floor of the tomb.

François de Laval was beatified in 1980; this means that, as a candidate for sainthood, he has reached the last stage before canonization, when a person is declared a saint. This can be a very long and complex process. Those promoting Bishop Laval's cause are hoping that God will give signs that he is worthy of being declared a saint. For example, a sick person might somehow be cured after invoking Bishop Laval, while praying before an image of him. If a doctor is willing to testify that he can find no natural explanation for what has taken place, then the authorities in Rome are asked to consider the case. Depending on the circumstances of the cures and the kinds of proofs available, more than one cure may be required.

The Sacred Congregation for the Causes of Saints is the body responsible for the process of beatification and canonization. For centuries, the most important officer of the Congregation was the Promoter of the Faith, (*Promotor Fidei*). It was his task to prepare arguments that could refute the proofs that had been brought forward. His popular title was the *Advocatus Diaboli*, or the "Devil's Advocate" - and that is the origin of this term, which we use in our daily speech today. In 1983, in an effort to simplify the process of canonization, Pope John Paul II approved changes that included abolition of the role of "Devil's Advocate."

BISHOP LAVAL'S DIOCESE: FROM QUEBEC TO THE GULF OF MEXICO

Bishop Laval's diocese covered most of North America north of the Spanish possessions in Mexico. In this reproduction of an early map, the profile of the east coast is relatively accurate, but it seems that the mapmaker became increasingly confused as he attempted to depict the centre of the continent, which the French were exploring at that time.

The prominence of the waterways is very striking in this depiction. In New France, almost all travel was done by water; the rivers were the highways linking the vast French territories in North America. The French colony of Louisiana is prominently indicated in the southern portion of the map. Using this extensive network of waterways it was possible to travel from Quebec City to New Orleans almost entirely by canoe.

SILVER

Notre-Dame de Québec has in its collection a remarkable 17th century vermeil chalice and paten which have been used to celebrate the Eucharist since the early days of the colony, when they were sent from France.

The paten, on which the host is placed, depicts the Coronation of the Virgin (right).

The chalice (below) is fashioned of vermeil, which means that it is made of sterling silver, coated with gold. The elaborate ornamentation features scenes from the life of the Virgin (below, right) and six standing angels presenting the instruments of the Passion.

SEMINARY OF QUEBEC

A VISION OF FRANCE IN NORTH AMERICA

I n 1663, the same year that Louis XIV made Quebec the capital of New France, François de Laval founded one of the most important institutions of the nascent colony, the Seminary of Quebec. His institution began as a community of diocesan priests, recruited in France to serve the population and help establish the first parishes. The priests – whose material needs were provided for by the Seminary – were sent out like soldiers from a barracks, staying for only brief periods of time in the homes of their parishioners. Thus, the

new settlers, who had challenges enough clearing the land for the first farms, did not have to deal with expense of a priest in residence.

In 1668, the priests established a second institution, the *Petit Séminaire*, to prepare young boys for the priesthood. While the boys lived in the Seminary, where they received a moral and spiritual education, they crossed the market square to attend the Jesuit College for their academic studies.

Continuity and Change

A CLASSICAL EDUCATION

The boys of the Seminary studied with the Jesuits until shortly after the conquest of 1759, when the Jesuit College was closed by the British and transformed into a barracks. Faced with the closing of this important educational institution, the priests of the Seminary decided, in 1765, to take over the teaching of academic subjects, offering a classical education to all boys with sufficient aptitude, not just those who were destined for the priesthood.

LAVAL UNIVERSITY

In 1852, the Seminary expanded its educational mandate once more with a very ambitious project: the founding of Laval University, the first French Catholic university in North America. Over the next hundred years, the university constructed buildings for its various faculties within the limited space available on the grounds of the Old Seminary, while gradually taking over houses in the surrounding neighbourhood, which became known as the Latin Quarter.

By the 1950s, however, it was becoming clear that the institution was putting too much pressure on the Old City, and Laval University began to move away from the upper town to a new campus in the modern suburb of Sainte-Foy. While many regretted the departure of the institution, problems would certainly have developed if the University had stayed in the historic area, with its densely packed buildings and narrow streets, and attempted to meet the needs of a growing educational community with parking requirements for thousands of students, professors and support staff.

THE SCHOOL OF ARCHITECTURE

Happily, since the end of the 1980s, certain parts of the university have returned to the older, downtown areas of Quebec City. Today, the school of architecture is housed in the oldest buildings of the Seminary, which were carefully restored and transformed for their new use in 1988-89. In 1994, The School of Visual Arts also moved to the central area of the city and is now located in a former factory building in the Saint-Roch quarter of the lower town. It is very appropriate that these creative disciplines in the university have returned to the city's central districts, with their inspiring historic architecture.

INDEPENDANT INSTITUTIONS

During the last decades of the 20th century, which saw rapid social change in the Province of Quebec, both Laval University and the *Pétit Séminaire* (now incorporated under the name Collège François-de-Laval) evolved into distinct entities which are completely separate from the Seminary that founded them. The College, a private high school that has been open to both girls and boys since 1989, now owns the buildings it occupies, some of which were originally built by the Seminary for Laval University. In 2008, Cardinal Marc Ouellet inaugurated a new *Petit Séminaire de Québec*, designed to prepare boys for the priesthood, but this more recent institution is not located within the historic Old Seminary.

THE SEMINARY FOR FOREIGN MISSIONS

The letters over the archway, SME, stand for the Séminaire des Missions étrangères, or Seminary for Foreign Missions, an institution which was established in Paris by friends of Bishop Laval in 1663. The objective of the Seminary for Foreign Missions was to spread the Catholic faith to faraway places like China and North America. In association with the institution in Paris, the Seminary of Quebec established missions to the east, that is, in Acadia (in regions now occupied by Nova Scotia and New Brunswick), and to the southwest, along the Mississippi Valley, as missionaries travelled with French explorers and voyageurs deep into the interior of the continent.

Architecture of New France

Entering into the Seminary courtyard (*below*), one feels as if one is no longer in North America. The Procure Wing, to the left, the oldest remaining building in the Seminary, was constructed in 1678. While it has undergone some modifications over time, the edifice still reflects the construction principles of the 17th and 18th centuries very well. It has a high steep roof, so that the snow slides off easily. The walls that rise above the roof line are fire walls – solid stone divisions that begin in the basement and project above the roofs so that, hopefully, fire is prevented from spreading from one part of the building to the next.

The thick stone walls are covered with a whitewashed mortar, called *crépi* in French. This protective covering is applied to stop water from entering cracks in the stones, where it can freeze and expand in the wintertime and thus damage the masonry. The courtyard of the Seminary gives us a good idea of what the entire city must have looked like at the time of New France, when the majority of the stone buildings were covered with whitewashed mortar.

COURTYARD AND GARDEN

Somewhat like an aristocratic residence in Paris, the Seminary has a courtyard side and a garden side. During the French régime, the Seminary garden, while not nearly as elaborate as the formal gardens of France, was nevertheless arranged in geometric patterns, in the French manner.

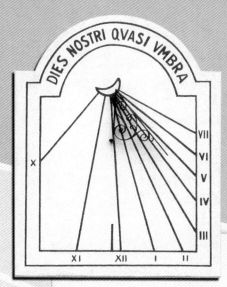

In French theatre, instead of saying "stage left - "stage right", as in English, people say "coté jardin" - "côté cour" (garden side and courtyard side). The origin of these terms goes back to a typical French organization of space, reflected here at the Seminary, as in the palaces and aristocratic residences, or "hôtels particuliers", built in Paris in the 17th and 18th centuries.

The garden side of the Procure Wing (*below*) is clad in wooden planks, a traditional method in Quebec to protect the masonry walls from northeasterly winds. Today, the Seminary's garden is greatly diminished. A considerable portion of the grounds came to be occupied by large buildings after the priests of the Seminary founded Laval University in 1852.

SUNDIAL

The sundial, which was installed on the courtyard façade of the Procure Wing in 1773, reminds us that human life is brief and that "our days flee like shadows."

External Chapel

(Chapel of the Museum of French North America)

Unlike the private interior chapels of the Seminary of Quebec, the External Chapel was a place of worship where all Catholics could pray and where the families and friends of priests and students were invited to attend religious ceremonies marking important moments in the life of the institution. The architect Joseph Ferdinand Peachy designed this building, which he constructed between 1888 and 1891, after a previous chapel was destroyed in a fire.

Peachy's plans were largely inspired by the Second Empire architecture of the *Église de la Trinité*, in Paris. The External Chapel of the Seminary, now part of the Museum of French North America, has been deconsecrated and is no longer a place of worship. Sacred objects are displayed in the former chapel, in which concerts and other events are often held. The ornate interior has a very interesting *trompe l'oeil* décor, in which metal-clad columns and other architectural elements were painted by the artist Wallace J. Fisher to give the impression that they are made of marble and granite.

RELICS OF THE SAINTS

The chapel is remarkable for the large collection of relics that it contains. Skulls, bones and locks of hair, as well as pieces of fabric that the saints are believed to have touched during their lifetimes, are displayed in containers called reliquaries. Mgr. Joseph-Calixte Marquis collected over 600 relics during his travels in Europe in the late 19th century. The Seminary possesses the largest collection of relics in Canada.

For generations, worshippers came here to venerate the remains of saints in hope of receiving indulgences. According to Catholic doctrine, these indulgences shortened the time that the faithful would have to spend in purgatory to expiate their sins, thus enabling them to reach heaven more quickly after their deaths. Posted by the original entrance door of this former chapel is a list of the indulgences that could be obtained by praying here. Although it was once a focus of great religious fervour in Quebec, the cult of relics has declined greatly since the 1950s.

ART AND FAITH

The main altarpiece (preceding page) is dominated by a sculpture of the Holy Family, the principal patron of the Seminary since its establishment by Bishop Laval in 1663. The altarpiece is made of fine marble and other precious materials, in contrast to the remarkably convincing trompe l'oeil background painted on the curved wall of the apse behind it to create the illusion of three-dimensional architectural elements and a tapestry suspended by rings.

Numerous relics (above, left) are displayed within little medallions, set in ornate gilded frames. These reliquaries are placed above secondary altars that were installed along the side aisles, so that the many priests of the Seminary could take turns celebrating private masses each day.

This reliquary (right), prominently located beside the main altar, contains the bones of Saint Clement, which were sent from Rome to Bishop Laval in 1677.

Lining the side aisles of the chapel are gilded busts (below), depicting the apostles, the four evangelists and Saint Paul, carved in wood by sculptor Louis Jobin in 1894–95. With great artistry, Jobin sought to capture the individual character of each saint. The sixteen busts are all reliquaries; beneath each sculpted portrait, a relic of the saint is displayed behind a pane of glass, framed by a wreath. Left to right: Saint Thomas, Saint Paul and Saint Mark.

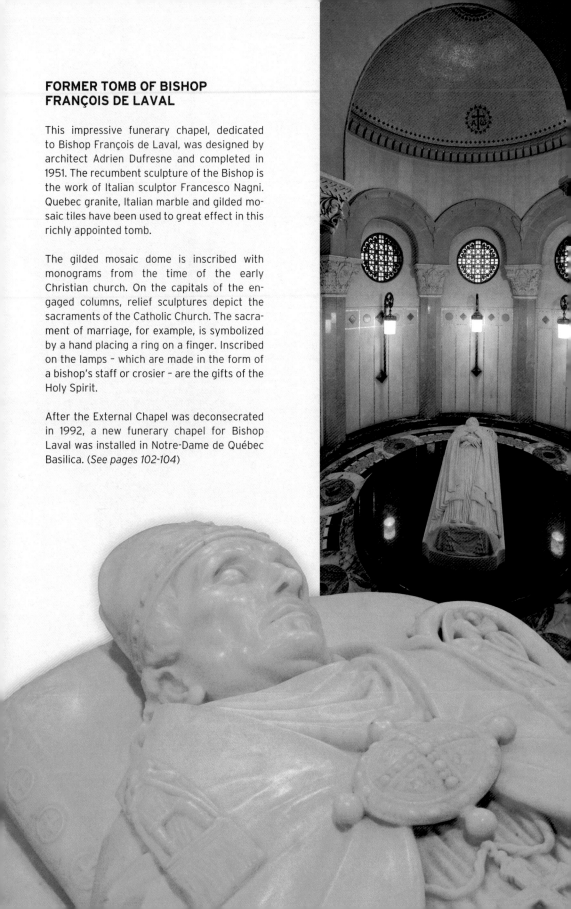

FORMER TOMB OF BISHOP FRANÇOIS DE LAVAL

This impressive funerary chapel, dedicated to Bishop François de Laval, was designed by architect Adrien Dufresne and completed in 1951. The recumbent sculpture of the Bishop is the work of Italian sculptor Francesco Nagni. Quebec granite, Italian marble and gilded mosaic tiles have been used to great effect in this richly appointed tomb.

The gilded mosaic dome is inscribed with monograms from the time of the early Christian church. On the capitals of the engaged columns, relief sculptures depict the sacraments of the Catholic Church. The sacrament of marriage, for example, is symbolized by a hand placing a ring on a finger. Inscribed on the lamps – which are made in the form of a bishop's staff or crosier – are the gifts of the Holy Spirit.

After the External Chapel was deconsecrated in 1992, a new funerary chapel for Bishop Laval was installed in Notre-Dame de Québec Basilica. (See pages 102-104)

INTERIOR CHAPELS

Monseigneur Briand's Chapel

The beautifully carved pine retable and Louis XV panelling of Bishop Jean-Olivier Briand's Chapel (top) were made by the talented cabinetmaker and sculptor Pierre Émond in 1785-86.

Chapel of the Congregation

The fine Neo-classical design of the Chapel of the Congregation (above right) is the work of Thomas Baillairgé, who worked closely with Abbé Jérôme Demers to renew church architecture in Quebec. Thomas Baillairgé sculpted all the statues and ornamentation in this chapel, in addition to drawing up the architectural plans. Later in his career he would delegate the actual sculpting to other craftsmen while he devoted himself more completely to the profession of architect. The career of Thomas Baillairgé (1791-1859) is a good illustration of how the métier of the skilled builder/artisan evolved into that of the more specialized professional architect in Quebec architectural history.

Exploring the Old Seminary

SAINT JOSEPH'S STAIRCASE

This beautiful wooden staircase (*left and right*), which leads to the vaulted basements of the Procure Wing, probably dates from the later part of the 18th century. The steps have been worn down by many generations of students.

VAULTED BASEMENTS

An impressive room (*below, left*) in the 17th century vaulted basement of the Procure Wing is known as "Bishop Laval's Kitchen." It contains a fireplace that is large enough to roast an ox. To build vaulted ceilings, skilled masons placed stone and mortar on specially prepared curved wooden frames. After the mortar dried the wooden support structure was removed, leaving stone arches which were extremely strong. Because of the solidity of these vaulted ceilings, citizens are said to have taken refuge here during sieges of the city. A vaulted stone corridor (*below, right*), leads to "Bishop Laval's Kitchen."

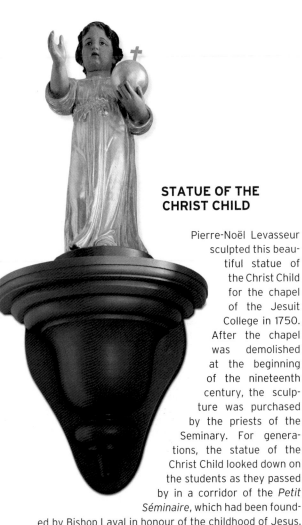

STATUE OF THE CHRIST CHILD

Pierre-Noël Levasseur sculpted this beautiful statue of the Christ Child for the chapel of the Jesuit College in 1750. After the chapel was demolished at the beginning of the nineteenth century, the sculpture was purchased by the priests of the Seminary. For generations, the statue of the Christ Child looked down on the students as they passed by in a corridor of the *Petit Séminaire*, which had been founded by Bishop Laval in honour of the childhood of Jesus. Today, the sculpture of the Christ Child – a special patron of the Seminary – has been given a place of honour beside the great staircase in the Priests' Residence.

AN EXTRAORDINARY STAIRCASE

This cast-iron staircase in the Priests' Residence was designed by Joseph Ferdinand Peachy in 1882. Because the stories in the Residence are of unequal height, it was a challenge to install this great structure. Remarkably, the builder whose skill and intelligence were crucial to the completion of this very complex project, a man by the name of Thomas Pampalon, was almost illiterate and had difficulty signing his own name.

The roof terrace of the Priests'
Residence offers a breathtaking
view. In the foreground is the
impressive mansard roof with lan-
tern towers added to the Central
Pavilion of Laval University
in 1875 by architect Joseph-
Ferdinand Peachy. In the background are the St. Lawrence River
and surrounding countryside. Left
to right: the Beauport and Beaupré
coasts, with the Laurentian
Mountains in distance; the Island
of Orleans; and the City of Lévis,
located on the south shore, across
the river from Quebec City.

CREDITS

Text and iconographic research: David Mendel
Photography: Luc-Antoine Couturier
English revision: Jane Macaulay
Graphic design: André Durocher (syclone.com)
Publisher and Project Coordinator: Sylvain Harvey
Printing: K2 Impressions
Public relations and Promotion: Véronique Bernier

Commission de la capitale nationale du Québec
Publishing Director: Denis Angers
Project Coordinator: Hélène Jean
Historian: Frédéric Smith
Archivist: Annik Cassista

First edition, 2009
© Éditions Sylvain Harvey and Commission de la
capitale nationale du Québec
ISBN 978-2-921703-84-0

Printed in Canada

Legal deposit – Bibliothèque et Archives nationales du
Québec, 2009
Legal deposit – Library and Archives Canada, 2009

Éditions Sylvain Harvey
Phone: (418) 692-1336 (Québec City area)
Toll-free: 1 800 476-2068 (Canada and U.S.A.)
E-mail: info@editionssylvainharvey.com
Website: www.editionssylvainharvey.com

Commission de la capitale nationale du Québec
Phone: (418) 528-0773
Toll-free: 1 800 442-0773
E-mail: commission@capitale.gouv.qc.ca
Website: www.capitale.gouv.qc.ca

Distribution in bookstores in Canada
Distribution Ulysse
Phone: (514) 843-9882, extension 2232
Toll-free: 1 800 748-9171
E-mail: info@ulysse.ca

We wish to thank the Société de développement des
entreprises culturelles du Québec (SODEC) for its aid
towards publishing, promotion and translation.

Government of Québec – Tax credit for book
publishing – Administered by SODEC

The publisher wishes to acknowledge the support of
the Canada Council for the Arts through the Book
Publishing Industry Development Program (BPIDP).

This book is also available in French under the title:
Québec, Ville du patrimoine mondial
ISBN: 978-2-921703-83-3

ACKNOWLEDGEMENTS

The author and photographer would like to express
their gratitude to all who opened their doors to us, mak-
ing accessible many hidden corners of the Old City: at
the Citadel of Quebec, Jocelyne Milot; at the Governor
General's Residence, Jocelyne Long, Laval Villeneuve
and Bertrand Pitre; at Parks Canada, Robert Gauvin
and Michel Brassard; at Fairmont le Château Frontenac,
Geneviève Parent, David Lessard, Steve Leblanc and
Micheline Dubé; at the Ursuline Convent of Quebec,
Sister Rita Michaud, Sister Marguerite Chénard, Sister
Gabrielle Noël and Sister Suzanne Prince; at the
Museum of the Ursuline Convent of Quebec, Christine
Cheyrou and Myriam Van Neste; at the Cathedral
of the Holy Trinity, Dean Walter Raymond, Jean
Thivièrge and Benjamin Waterhouse; at Notre-Dame
de Québec, Chanoine Jean-Marie Chamberland and
Patrick McGinnis; at the Corporation du Patrimoine et
du Tourisme religieux, Sarah Michelle Couillard, Francis
Jacques, Annie Blouin and Marie-Christine Joly; at
the Seminary of Quebec, Abbé Jacques Roberge; at
the Laval University School of Architecture, Laurent
Goulard; at the Museum of French North America,
Claire Simard, Danielle Aubin and Serge Poulin; at the
Collège François-de-Laval, Réjean Lemay.

Our thanks to the archivists who provided access to images from the past, allowing the reader to travel back in
time and see the places of today in a wider context.

Thanks as well to those who offered help, informa-
tion, ideas and inspiration along the way: Jean-Paul
L'Allier, Barry Lane, Denis Martin, Pierre Lahoud,
Claude Paulette, Claude Payeur, Gino Gariépy, Christina
Laroux, Réginald Auger, Marcel Moussette, Kate Reed,
Clive Meredith, Rosemary Bachelor, Joanna Foust,
Donna McEwen and Josée Savard.

Our sincere gratitude to the team whose combined tal-
ent, determination, and effort made it possible to transform the ephemeral experience of a guided tour into
this book: publisher, Sylvain Harvey; designer, André
Durocher; English revision, Jane Macaulay; French revision, Carole Noël; translation, Paule Champoux; promotion, Véronique Bernier; and, at the Commission de
la capitale nationale du Québec, Denis Angers, Hélène
Jean, Annik Cassista and Frédéric Smith.

ILLUSTRATION CREDITS

P. 8 - Quebec from the Citadel, by Philip John
Bainbrigge, 1836, Royal Ontario Museum. P. 10 - Map
showing the rescue effort in September 1729 by the

Governor of New France, the Marquis of Beauharnois, at the time of the shipwreck of the *Éléphant* between Quebec and the Island of Orleans, by Mahier, 1729, Bibliothèque nationale de France (GED 7825 RES). P. 11 - Map of North America, by Jean-Baptiste Franquelin, 1688, Bibliothèque et archives nationales du Québec, (ORIGINAL: Service historique de la marine, Bibliothèque centrale de Vincennes, France) (E6,S7,SS1,P6820177). P. 12-13 - *The Death of General Wolfe*, by Benjamin West, 1770, National Gallery of Canada. P. 14 - Sillery Cove, looking towards Pointe-a-Pizeau, by John Thompson, 1891, Bibliothèque et archives nationales du Québec (C006073). P. 18 - Michel Particelli d'Emery, by Balthazar Moncornet, 1654, Bibliothèque nationale de France, (C56340). P. 18 - Samuel de Champlain, attributed to Louis-César-Joseph Ducornet, 1854, Bibliothèque et archives nationales du Québec, (P600,S5,PIC43). P. 22 - Map of Québec, by Jean Bourdon, 1664, Library and Archives Canada. P. 22 - Château Frontenac and Place d'Armes, aerial photograph by Pierre Lahoud. P. 24 - *View of the Cathedral, Jesuits College and Recollet Friars Church*, by Richard Short, 1759, engraved by P. Canot, 1761, McCord Museum, (M970.67.11). P. 24 - *The Quebec Driving Club meeting at the Place d'Armes*, by James Smillie, after Ensign William Wallace, 1826, The Peter Winkworth Collection of Canadiana, Library and Archives Canada. P. 28 - Château Frontenac, photographer unknown, c. 1922, Bibliothèque et archives nationales du Québec. P. 29 - Map detail, 1895, Canadian Pacific Archives (A6528). P. 29 - *The White Empresses of the Pacific*, 1932, Canadian Pacific Archives (A6024). P. 29 - *Empress Steamers and Only Four Days Open Sea*, Canadian Pacific Archives (A.6352). P. 36 - The Earl of Athlone, President Frankin D. Roosevelt, and the Rt. Hons. Winston Churchill and W.L. Mackenzie King during the Octagon Conference, 1944, National Film Board of Canada, Library and Archives Canada. P. 39 - Dufferin Terrace in Summer, by Hethrington, c.1900, Bibliothèque et archives nationales du Québec, (E6,S8,P276). P. 42 - Plans and elevations of the Château Saint-Louis in the City of Quebec, 10 July 1724, Archives nationales de France (FR CAOM 03DFC408B). P. 42 - 18th century French wine bottle, Parks Canada (38G30D37-2Q), photograph by Luc-Antoine Couturier. P. 43 - Icehouse dating from 1771, Parks Canada (38G86R1 35X04), photograph by Michel Élie. P. 48 - *Monument to Wolfe and Montcalm*, James Pattison Cockburn, 1828-1832, National Gallery of Canada, Ottawa. P. 65 - Detail of embroidery, Nativity Altar Frontal, Musée des Ursulines de Québec, Collection of the Monastery of the Ursulines of Quebec (1995.63), photograph by Patrick Altman. P. 68 - Plan of the City and Château of Quebec, by Villeneuve, 1685, Archives nationales d'Outre-Mer (FRANOM_03DFC3498B). P. 69 - Bird's-eye view of the corner of Donnacona and Des Jardins Streets, photograph by David Mendel. P. 84 - Upper town market, by Louis-Prudent Vallée, 1869, Bibliothèque et archives nationales du Québec (E6,S8,P404). P. 88 - *A View of the Jesuits College and Church*, by Richard Short, 1759, engraved by C. Grignion, 1761, McCord Museum, (M970.67.7).

FURTHER READING

Among the many excellent books that have been written about Quebec City I would like to suggest certain key publications. Two of the best guidebooks are *An Historical Guide to Quebec*, by Yves Tessier (Québec: Société historique de Québec et la Commission de la capitale nationale du Québec, 2005), and *Le Vieux-Quebec, Guide du promeneur*, by Jean-Marie Lebel (Sillery: Éditions du Septentrion, 1997). Quebec City's 400th anniversary was a banner year for books on the city's history, including *Québec, quatre siècles d'une capitale*, by Christian Blais, Gilles Gallichan, Frédéric Lemieux and Jocelyn Saint-Pierre (Québec: Les Publications du Québec, 2008); *L'histoire du Vieux-Québec à travers son patrimoine*, by Jean Provencher (Quebec: Les Publications du Québec, 2008), and *Histoire de Québec et de sa région*, by Marc Vallières, Yvon Desloges and Fernand Harvey (Québec: Les Presses de l'Université Laval, 2008). For the architecture of the city, read *Québec, trois siècles d'architecture*, by Luc Noppen, Claude Paulette and Michel Tremblay (Québec: Libre Expression and Les Publications du Québec, 1979), and *Québec, de roc et de pierre, la capitale en architecture*, by Luc Noppen and Lucie K. Morisset (Sainte-Foy: Éditions Multimondes and Commission de la capitale nationale du Québec, 1998). For British influences, read *The Anglos, The Hidden Face of Quebec City*, by Louisa Blair (Québec: Éditions Sylvain Harvey and Commission de la capitale nationale du Québec, 2005). For the city in works of art, read *Québec : Recueil Iconographique, A Pictorial Record, 1608-1875*, by Charles P. De Volpi (Toronto: Longman Canada, 1971), and *Québec, une ville et ses artistes*, under the direction of Denis Castonguay and Yves Lacasse (Québec: Musée national des beaux-arts du Québec, 2008). For archaeology, read *Québec, la ville sous la ville*, by Denis Roy and Hélène Déslauriers (Québec: Ville de Québec, 1987). On Champlain and his portraits, read *Portraits des héros de la Nouvelle-France, images d'un culte historique*, by Denis Martin (LaSalle: Éditions Hurtubise, HMH, 1988).